GAO

Report to the Chairman, Committee on Oversight and Government Reform, House of Representatives

I0426425

March 2012

INFORMATION TECHNOLOGY

FDA Needs to Fully Implement Key Management Practices to Lessen Modernization Risks

GAO

Accountability ★ Integrity ★ Reliability

March 2012

INFORMATION TECHNOLOGY

FDA Needs to Fully Implement Key Management Practices to Lessen Modernization Risks

Highlights of GAO-12-346, a report to the Chairman, Committee on Oversight and Government Reform, House of Representatives

Why GAO Did This Study

The Food and Drug Administration (FDA), an agency within the Department of Health and Human Services (HHS), relies heavily on information technology (IT) to carry out its mission of ensuring the safety and effectiveness of regulated consumer products. Specifically, IT systems are critical to FDA's product review, adverse event reporting, and compliance activities. Recognizing limitations in its IT capabilities, the agency has undertaken various initiatives to modernize its systems. GAO was asked to (1) assess FDA's current portfolio of IT systems, including the number of systems in use and under development, and their purpose and costs; (2) assess the status and effectiveness of FDA's efforts to modernize the mission-critical systems that support its regulatory programs; and (3) examine the agency's progress in effectively integrating and sharing data among key systems. To do this, GAO reviewed information on key FDA systems and interviewed agency officials to determine the status of systems and the effectiveness of key IT management practices, as well as data sharing among key systems.

What GAO Recommends

GAO is recommending that FDA develop a comprehensive inventory of its IT systems, develop an integrated master schedule for a major modernization effort, and assess information needs to identify opportunities for greater sharing. In commenting on a draft of this report, HHS neither agreed nor disagreed with the recommendations but stated that FDA has taken actions to address many of the issues in the report.

View GAO-12-346. For more information, contact Valerie C. Melvin, (202) 512-6304 or melvinv@gao.gov.

What GAO Found

While FDA has taken several important steps toward modernizing its IT environment, much remains to be done. FDA reported spending about $400 million for IT investments in fiscal year 2011; however, the agency currently lacks a comprehensive IT inventory that identifies and provides key information about the systems it uses and is developing. Office of Management and Budget (OMB) and GAO guidance call for federal agencies to maintain such an inventory in order to monitor and manage their IT investments. This inventory should include information on each system, such as costs, functionality or purpose, and status. However, FDA does not have such a comprehensive list of its systems. Instead, the agency points to budget documents required by OMB, which included information on 44 IT investments for fiscal year 2011. The agency also provided a partial list of 21 mission-critical systems and modernization initiatives. Nonetheless, agency officials acknowledged that these documents do not identify all FDA's systems or the complete costs, purpose, or status of each system. Until the agency has a complete and comprehensive inventory, it will lack critical information needed to effectively assess its IT portfolio.

Much work remains on FDA's largest and costliest system modernization effort—the Mission Accomplishments and Regulatory Compliance Services program. This program is estimated to cost about $280 million and is intended to enhance existing applications and develop new systems that provide information for inspections, compliance activities, and laboratory operations. However, much of the planned functionality has not been delivered and its completion is uncertain. Moreover, the program lacks an integrated master schedule identifying all the work activities that need to be performed and their interdependencies. FDA's Chief Information Officer (CIO) stated that the agency is reevaluating the scope of the initiative. As a result, it is uncertain when or if FDA will meet its goals of replacing key legacy systems and providing modernized functionality to support its mission. In addition, FDA has not yet fully implemented key IT management capabilities essential for successful modernization, as previously recommended by GAO. These include developing an actionable IT strategic plan, developing an enterprise architecture to guide its modernization effort, and assessing its IT human capital needs. This is due in part to the fact that FDA's IT management structure has been in flux. Since 2008, the agency has had five CIOs, hampering its ability to plan and effectively implement a long-range IT strategy. While the agency recently hired a CIO, without stable leadership and capabilities, the success of FDA's modernization efforts is in jeopardy.

The agency currently has initiatives under way to improve its data sharing with internal and external partners, including adoption of an enterprisewide standard for formatting data and several projects aimed at enhancing its ability to share data. Effective data sharing is essential to its review and approval process, inspection of imports and manufacturing facilities, and tracking of contaminated products. However, these projects have made mixed progress, and significant work remains for FDA to fully implement standardized data sharing. Further, FDA's Center for Food Safety and Applied Nutrition has not comprehensively assessed information-sharing needs to ensure that its systems and databases are organized for effective information sharing. This is needed to help ensure more efficient access to and sharing of key information supporting its mission.

_____ United States Government Accountability Office

Contents

Tables

Figures

Abbreviations

CFSAN	Center for Food Safety and Applied Nutrition
CIO	Chief Information Officer
FACTS	Field Accomplishments and Compliance Tracking System
FDA	Food and Drug Administration
HHS	Department of Health and Human Services
HL7	Health Level Seven
ICT21	Information and Computing Technologies for the 21st Century
IMS	integrated master schedule
IT	information technology
MARCS	Mission Accomplishments and Regulatory Compliance Services
OASIS	Operational and Administrative System for Import Support
OIM	Office of Information Management
OMB	Office of Management and Budget
ORA	Office of Regulatory Affairs
PREDICT	Predictive Risk-based Evaluation for Dynamic Import Compliance Targeting

March 15, 2012

The Honorable Darrell Issa
Chairman
Committee on Oversight and Government Reform
House of Representatives

Dear Mr. Chairman:

The Food and Drug Administration (FDA) is responsible for ensuring the safety of a wide range of consumer products, including approximately 80 percent of our nation's food supply.[1] FDA's regulatory program includes premarket reviews of drug and medical products; inspections of manufacturers; and postmarket surveillance of food, drug, and medical products.

In carrying out these responsibilities, the agency relies heavily on information technology (IT). Specifically, IT systems are critical to the agency's product review, adverse event reporting, and compliance activities. However, reports on the agency's IT that we, FDA's Science Board,[2] and others[3] have previously issued noted limitations in a number of key areas, including data availability and quality, the reliability and redundancy of the agency's infrastructure, and its ability to use technology to improve regulatory effectiveness. These limitations have

---

[1]FDA Science Board, *FDA Science and Mission at Risk* (Rockville, Md.: November 2007).The Department of Agriculture regulates meat, poultry, and some egg products. FDA regulates drug residues that may be present in edible products derived from treated animals (including meat, milk, and eggs).

[2]The Science Board to the FDA consists of 21 members selected by the Commissioner or designee from among authorities knowledgeable in the fields of food safety, nutrition, chemistry, pharmacology, toxicology, clinical research or systems biology, health care devices, nanotechnology, medical imaging, robotics, cell- and tissue-based products, regenerative medicine, and combination products. The Science Board provides advice primarily to the Commissioner and other appropriate officials on specific complex and technical issues, as well as emerging issues within the scientific community, in industry and academia.

[3]Deloitte Consulting, *Food and Drug Administration: Enterprise Information Management Strategy* (Atlanta, Ga.: Dec. 10, 2007). Breckenridge Institute, Independent Verification and Validation of AERS I Requirements Process (Breckenridge, Colo.: November 2006).

persisted even as the agency has undertaken various initiatives to modernize its IT systems.

Given the importance of IT to the agency's ability to effectively fulfill its mission, you asked us to (1) assess FDA's current portfolio of IT systems, including the number of systems in use and under development, and their purpose and costs; (2) assess the status and effectiveness of FDA's efforts to modernize the mission-critical systems that support its regulatory program; and (3) examine the agency's progress in effectively integrating and sharing data among key systems.

To assess the portfolio of IT systems, we reviewed agency documentation identifying key systems, including FDA's plans for modernizing its IT infrastructure and administrative processes, a list of systems that the agency identified as mission critical, and the agency's Office of Management and Budget (OMB) exhibit 300s[4] and exhibit 53s.[5] We examined these documents to determine if the list provided was comprehensive and included critical information, such as purpose and costs, required to effectively manage a large investment portfolio. We also interviewed officials regarding management of the agency's IT investments.

To assess the status and effectiveness of FDA's efforts to modernize its mission-critical systems, we reviewed the FDA Science Board study and reports that we and others have issued to identify shortfalls in the agency's systems that are intended to support regulatory programs. We interviewed relevant agency officials regarding the status of initiatives and plans to modernize mission-critical systems, including the Office of Regulatory Affairs' (ORA) Mission Accomplishments and Regulatory Compliance Services (MARCS) legacy systems replacement program. We analyzed key documents reflecting the MARCS project scope and modernization approach to determine whether the effort will accomplish the agency's goals of replacing legacy systems that support its regulatory mission. We also reviewed MARCS modernization plans to determine if

---

[4]Each year, agencies submit to OMB a Capital Asset Plan and Business Case—the exhibit 300—to justify each request for a major IT investment.

[5]Each federal agency reports its IT Investment Portfolio annually to OMB via an exhibit 53. The exhibit 53 provides budget estimates for all IT investments and identifies those that are major investments. OMB uses the exhibit 53 to create an overall "Federal IT Investment Portfolio" published as part of the President's Budget.

the agency is following best practices for development of an integrated master schedule (IMS) to plan and manage the effort. In addition, we visited FDA facilities at the Port of Baltimore in Baltimore, Maryland, to observe a demonstration of new capabilities to screen imports that were in part provided by MARCS. Further, we assessed FDA's progress in addressing prior GAO recommendations related to the implementation of key IT management practices (IT strategic planning, developing and implementing an enterprise architecture, and IT human capital management) by interviewing relevant agency officials and analyzing key supporting documentation.

To determine the agency's progress in effectively integrating and sharing data among key systems, we reviewed project plans, schedules, and other documents describing FDA's plans to implement a standard adopted enterprisewide for the exchange and analysis of information—Health Level Seven (HL7).[6] We also reviewed agency documentation describing the progress of additional projects intended to enhance the agency's ability to share data. Further, we selected FDA's Center for Food Safety and Applied Nutrition (CFSAN) to assess sharing across databases supporting FDA's regulatory mission because of previously identified deficiencies in specific functions, such as sharing information on recalls of contaminated foods.[7] We analyzed the number of databases, their purposes, and corresponding IT systems used by CFSAN to conduct its regulatory work, and assessed the efforts and methodology used by the center to improve information sharing and exchange between databases against OMB and federal Chief Information Officer Council guidance. We supplemented our review with information from CFSAN and Office of Information Management (OIM) officials regarding efforts to improve data sharing and interoperability of systems.

---

[6]FDA has adopted the HL7 international healthcare informatics interoperability standard as its single data model to facilitate a common understanding between the data submitter and user.

[7]GAO, *Food Labeling: FDA Needs to Better Leverage Resources, Improve Oversight, and Effectively Use Available Data to Help Consumers Select Healthy Foods*, GAO-08-597 (Washington, D.C.: Sept. 9, 2008); *Seafood Fraud: FDA Program Changes and Better Collaboration among Key Federal Agencies Could Improve Detection and Prevention*, GAO-09-258 (Washington, D.C.: Feb. 19, 2009); and *Food Safety: FDA Could Strengthen Oversight of Imported Food by Improving Enforcement and Seeking Additional Authorities*, GAO-10-699T (Washington, D.C.: May 6, 2010).

We conducted this performance audit at FDA headquarters in White Oak, Maryland, from March 2011 to March 2012 in accordance with generally accepted government auditing standards. Those standards require that we plan and perform the audit to obtain sufficient, appropriate evidence to provide a reasonable basis for our findings and conclusions based on our audit objectives. We believe that the evidence obtained provides a reasonable basis for our findings and conclusions based on our audit objectives. For more details on our objectives, scope, and methodology, see appendix I.

Background

An agency within the U.S. Department of Health and Human Services (HHS), FDA is responsible for promoting and protecting the public health by ensuring the safety, efficacy, and security of human and veterinary drugs, biological products, and medical devices, and ensuring the safety and security of our nation's food supply, cosmetics, and products that emit radiation. The agency is also responsible for ensuring the proper labeling of foods, drugs, medical devices, tobacco, and cosmetics. Its work also includes advancing public health by facilitating innovations and promoting public access to science-based information on medicines, devices, and foods. The agency does not regulate meat, poultry, and certain egg products, which are regulated by the U.S. Department of Agriculture.[8]

FDA performs regulatory activities that include

- reviewing and approving new drugs and certain medical products;

- inspecting manufacturing facilities for compliance with regulations and good manufacturing practices; and

- conducting postmarket surveillance of food, drug, and medical products to ensure that products are safe; tracking and identifying the source of outbreaks of foodborne illnesses; and issuing recall notices and safety alerts for products that threaten the public health.

FDA exercises its core functions through four directorates: the Offices of Medical Products and Tobacco; Foods; Global Regulatory Operations

---

[8]FDA regulates drug residues that may be present in edible products derived from treated animals (including meat, milk, and eggs).

and Policy; and Operations. These offices, along with the Office of the Chief Scientist, report to the FDA Commissioner and carry out their missions through seven centers and through FDA's ORA.

Office of Medical Products and Tobacco:

- *Center for Biologics Evaluation and Research.* Regulates and evaluates the safety and effectiveness of biological products, such as blood and blood products, vaccines and allergenic products, and protein-based drugs.

- *Center for Drug Evaluation and Research.* Promotes and protects the public health by ensuring that all prescription and over-the-counter drugs are safe, as well as by reviewing and regulating clinical research.

- *Center for Devices and Radiological Health.* Promotes and protects the public health by ensuring the safety and effectiveness of medical devices and preventing unnecessary human exposure to radiation from radiation-emitting products.

- *Center for Tobacco Products.* Oversees tobacco product performance standards, reviews premarket applications for new and modified risk tobacco products and new warning labels, and establishes and enforces advertising and promotion restrictions.

Office of Foods:

- *Center for Food Safety and Applied Nutrition.* In conjunction with FDA's field staff, promotes and protects the public health, in part by ensuring the safety of the food supply and that foods are properly labeled, and ensures that cosmetics are safe and properly labeled.

- *Center for Veterinary Medicine.* Promotes and protects the public health and animal health by helping to ensure that animal food products are safe; and by evaluating the safety and effectiveness of drugs to treat companion animals and those used for food-producing animals.

Office of the Commissioner:

- *National Center for Toxicological Research.* Conducts peer-reviewed scientific research and provides expert technical advice and training to support FDA's science-based regulatory decisions.

Office of Global Regulatory Operations and Policy:

- *Office of Regulatory Affairs.* Leads FDA field activities and provides FDA leadership on imports, inspections, and enforcement policy. ORA supports the FDA product centers by inspecting regulated products and manufacturers, conducting sample analysis on regulated products, and reviewing imported products offered for entry into the United States. The office also develops FDA-wide policy on compliance and enforcement and executes FDA's Import Strategy and Food Protection Plans.

FDA's Reliance on IT

FDA relies extensively on IT to fulfill its mission and to support related administrative needs. The agency has systems dedicated to supporting the following major mission activities:

- *Reviewing and evaluating new product applications, such as for prescription drugs, medical devices, and food additives.* These systems are intended to help FDA determine whether a product is safe before it enters the market. For example, the Document Archiving, Reporting, and Regulatory Tracking System is intended to manage the drug and therapeutics review process.

- *Tracking and evaluating firms to ensure that products comply with regulatory requirements.* For example, the Field Accomplishments and Compliance Tracking System (FACTS) supports inspections, investigations, and compliance activities.

- *Monitoring the safety of products on the market by collecting and assessing adverse reactions to FDA-regulated products, such as illnesses due to food or negative reactions to drugs.* For example, the Vaccine Adverse Event Reporting System accepts reports of adverse events that may be associated with U.S.-licensed vaccines from health care providers, manufacturers, and the public.

In addition, FDA relies on various systems that support its administrative processes, such as payroll administration and personnel systems. All of the agency's systems are supported by an IT infrastructure that includes network components, critical servers, and multiple data centers.

The information that FDA receives is growing in volume and complexity. According to the agency, from 2001 to 2011, the number of import shipments that it inspected for admission into the United States increased from about 7 million imports reviewed annually to over 22.6 million. Additionally, in 2011, the agency estimated that 15 percent of the U.S. food supply was imported, including 60 percent of fresh fruits and vegetables and 80 percent of seafood. Advances in science and the increase in imports are factors affecting the complexity of information that FDA receives. The ability of the agency's IT systems and infrastructure to accommodate this growth is crucial to FDA's ability to accomplish its mission effectively.

Compounding these challenges, reports and studies, both by FDA and others, have noted limitations in a number of key aspects of FDA's IT environment, including data availability and quality, IT infrastructure, the agency's ability to use technology to improve regulatory effectiveness, and IT management. In 2007, the FDA Science Board issued a report, *FDA Science and Mission at Risk*,[9] which provided a broad assessment of challenges facing the agency. Specifically, this study found that the agency's IT infrastructure was outdated and unstable, and it lacked sufficient controls to ensure continuity of operations or to provide effective disaster recovery services. The Science Board also stated that the agency did not have sufficient IT staff with skills in such areas as capital planning/investment control and enterprise architecture; that processes for recruitment and retention of IT staff were inadequate; and that the agency did not invest sufficiently in professional development. Further, the Science Board found that information was not easily and immediately accessible throughout the agency (including critical clinical trial data that were available only in paper form), hampering FDA's ability to regulate products. Data and information exchange was impeded because information resided in different systems that were not integrated. According to the Science Board, FDA lacked sufficient standards for data exchanges, both within the agency and between the agency and external parties, reducing its capability to manage the complex data and

---

[9]FDA Science Board, *FDA Science and Mission at Risk* (Rockville, Md.: November 2007).

information challenges associated with rapid innovation, such as new data types, data models, and analytic methods.

Also in 2007, FDA commissioned Deloitte Consulting, LLP, to examine ways in which the agency could better meet increased demand for information and make decisions more quickly and easily. Deloitte's study stated that FDA needed to develop both a common enterprise information management architecture and an IT architecture to facilitate both short-term operational gains, such as improved information access, and long-term gains in strategic flexibility. Deloitte noted that FDA's former decentralized approach to IT, in which the centers developed their own systems, had led to duplicative work efforts, tools, and information.

Prior GAO Reports Have Highlighted Challenges with FDA's IT Systems and Modernization Efforts

We also have previously reported on FDA's systems and modernization efforts and noted deficiencies in its IT management. For example, in a June 2009 report on the agency's plans for modernizing its IT systems,[10] we noted that FDA lacked a comprehensive IT strategic plan that included results-oriented goals and performance measures to guide the agency's modernization projects and activities. We also pointed out that FDA had made mixed progress in establishing important IT management capabilities that are essential in helping ensure a successful modernization. These capabilities included investment management, information security, enterprise architecture development, and human capital management. To help ensure the success of the agency's modernization efforts, we recommended that it expeditiously develop a comprehensive IT strategic plan, give priority to architecture development, and complete key elements of its IT human capital planning. FDA agreed with our recommendations and identified actions initiated or planned to address them.

In addition, we have previously identified problems with FDA's Operational and Administrative System for Import Support (OASIS) import-screening system. Specifically, we reported in 2008 that OASIS had an inaccurate count of foreign establishments manufacturing drugs because unreliable manufacturer identification numbers were generated

---

[10]GAO, *Information Technology: FDA Needs to Establish Key Plans and Processes for Guiding Systems Modernization Efforts*, GAO-09-523 (Washington, D.C.: June 2, 2009).

by customs brokers.[11] FDA officials said these errors resulted in the creation of multiple records for a single establishment, which led to inflated counts of establishments offering drugs for import into the U.S. market. While FDA officials acknowledged this problem, they were unable to provide us with an estimate of the extent of these errors. In addition, the agency did not have a process for systematically identifying and correcting these errors. Accordingly, we made recommendations aimed at correcting these deficiencies; however, FDA did not comment on these recommendations. In September 2010, we reported that OASIS still provided an inaccurate count of foreign establishments manufacturing drugs offered for import into the United States.[12]

Further, in September 2009, we reported that Customs and Border Protection's import screening system did not notify OASIS when imported food shipments arrived at U.S. ports.[13] We pointed out that, without access to time-of-arrival information, FDA did not know when shipments that require examinations or reinspections arrive at the port, which could increase the risk that unsafe food may enter U.S. commerce. We therefore recommended that Customs and Border Protection ensure that its new screening system communicates time-of-arrival information to FDA, and the agency agreed with this recommendation. In May 2010, we testified that, according to FDA officials, Customs and Border Protection had modified its software to notify FDA of a shipment's time of arrival.[14]

In addition, we previously identified deficiencies in sharing information related to food products. In September 2008, we reported that FDA did not have reliable data on the number of food labels reviewed, and that the agency did not track the timely correction of labeling violations.[15] We made recommendations to correct these deficiencies, but FDA did not

---

[11]GAO, *Drug Safety: Better Data Management and More Inspections Are Needed to Strengthen FDA's Foreign Drug Inspection Program*, GAO-08-970 (Washington, D.C.: Sept. 22, 2008).

[12]GAO, *Drug Safety: FDA Has Conducted More Foreign Inspections and Begun to Improve Its Information on Foreign Establishments, but More Progress Is Needed*, GAO-10-961 (Washington, D.C.: Sept. 30, 2010).

[13]GAO, *Food Safety: Agencies Need to Address Gaps in Enforcement and Collaboration to Enhance Safety of Imported Food*, GAO-09-873 (Washington, D.C.: Sept. 15, 2009).

[14]GAO-10-699T.

[15]GAO-08-597.

commit to taking action on them. Further, in February 2009, we reported that Customs and Border Protection, the National Marine Fishery Service, and FDA each collected information on seafood products to meet their respective responsibilities, but did not effectively share information that could be used to detect and prevent inaccurate labeling of seafood.[16] As a result, we recommended that the three agencies develop goals, strategies, and mechanisms for interagency information sharing, which the agencies generally agreed with. Finally, in May 2010, we testified that the lack of a unique identifier for firms exporting food products may have allowed contaminated food to evade FDA's review, and that the agency did not always share information on food distribution lists with states. We pointed out that this impeded states' efforts to remove contaminated products from grocery stores and warehouses.[17]

IT Organizational Structure and Governance

Driven in part by the various studies of the agency's IT environment, in May 2008 FDA transitioned to an enterprisewide approach to IT management. Prior to this transition, the agency's IT management was decentralized, with each center having its own Office of Technology. According to FDA officials, this led to an environment in which systems did not interoperate and were often redundant and investment in IT infrastructure and systems development was inadequate.

In moving to an enterprisewide approach, the agency transferred responsibility for managing IT from individual components (centers and ORA) to a new centralized Office of Information Management (OIM). OIM resides within FDA's Office of Operations and is headed by the Chief Information Officer (CIO).[18] The CIO reports to the agency's Chief Operating Officer. As head of OIM, the CIO is responsible for managing IT, creating a foundation to enhance the interoperability of systems, and managing more than 400 staff assigned to this office.

OIM is composed of five divisions: Business Partnership and Support, Systems Management, Infrastructure Operations, Technology, and Chief

---

[16]GAO-09-258.

[17]GAO-10-699T.

[18]The CIO has a dual role and is also the Chief Scientist of Informatics.

Information Officer Support. It is responsible for managing IT and other related services enterprisewide. This includes

- developing the architecture, standards, policies, governance, best practices, and technology road map that support the business priorities of the agency, including managing IT infrastructure, telecommunications, security, business continuity and disaster recovery, strategic planning, capital planning and investment control, enterprise architecture, and applications development and management;

- advising and providing assistance to the FDA Commissioner and senior management officials on IT resources and programs;

- establishing and overseeing implementation of agency IT policy and governance, procedures, and processes for conformance with the Clinger-Cohen Act and the Paperwork Reduction Act; and

- working with FDA business areas to develop and communicate the overall vision for the agency's IT program.

In early March 2012, the CIO began developing a new Project Management Office.[19] As part of this office, an Interim Informatics Governance Board is expected to perform investment evaluations and project assessments. FDA's senior executive team, which is comprised of the Deputy Commissioners, the Associate Commissioner for Regulatory Affairs, Center Directors, and the CIO, is responsible for governance of all IT investments.

---

[19]According to the CIO, this office will be implemented in March 2012 and focus on IT planning, budgeting, acquisitions, and training.

FDA's IT Budget

FDA received about $418 million in IT funding for fiscal year 2012. For fiscal year 2011, the agency's IT budget was approximately $439 million, as illustrated in figure 1.

Figure 1: FDA IT Funding Levels for FY2008 through FY2012

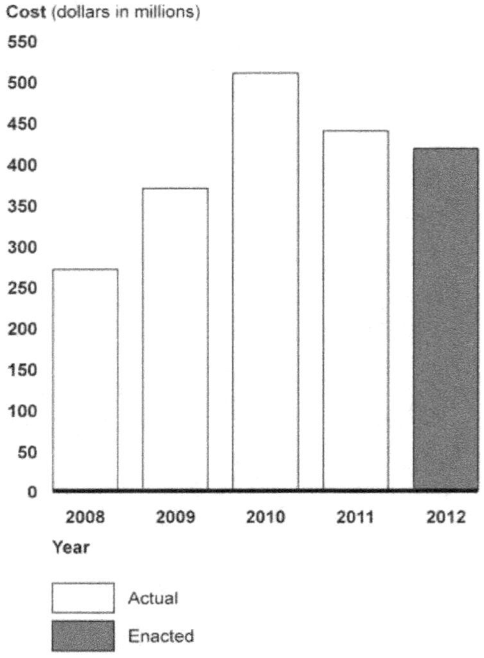

Cost (dollars in millions)

Year	Value
2008	~270 (Actual)
2009	~370 (Actual)
2010	~510 (Actual)
2011	~440 (Actual)
2012	~418 (Enacted)

Legend:
- Actual
- Enacted

Source: FDA data.

As illustrated in figure 2, about 60 percent of FDA's reported IT costs in fiscal year 2011 supported IT operations and infrastructure, such as network servers, telecommunications, and computers, with the remaining 40 percent supporting the development and modernization of IT systems.

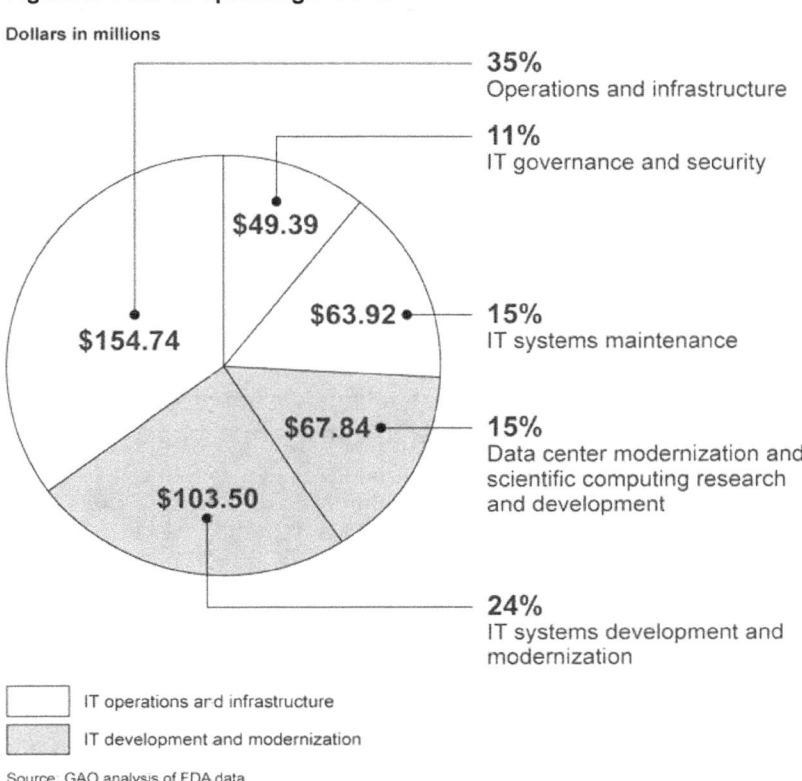

Figure 2: Total IT Spending FY2011

Dollars in millions

35%
Operations and infrastructure

11%
IT governance and security

$49.39

$63.92 • 15%
IT systems maintenance

$154.74

$67.84 • 15%
Data center modernization and
scientific computing research
and development

$103.50

24%
IT systems development and
modernization

☐ IT operations and infrastructure

▨ IT development and modernization

Source: GAO analysis of FDA data.

FDA Lacks a Comprehensive List of Its IT Systems

Federal guidance calls for agencies to prepare and maintain a comprehensive list of their IT systems. Specifically, OMB Circular No. A-130 guidance calls for a complete inventory of agency information, to include identifying and describing information services, such as systems and databases, used throughout the agency. In addition, GAO's IT investment management framework,[20] stresses that a foundational practice for effectively managing an organization's investments is having an up-to-date and complete collection of information on its assets, including systems, software applications and tools, and licensing

---

[20]GAO, *Information Technology Investment Management: A Framework for Assessing and Improving Process Maturity*, Version 1.1, GAO-04-394G (Washington, D.C.: March 2004).

agreements. According to the framework, to make good investment decisions, an organization should maintain pertinent information about each investment and store that information in a retrievable format, such as a central repository, to be used in future investment decisions. Such a repository is to include, among other things, the current life cycle phase of the system; the responsible organizational unit; the costs to date and anticipated future costs; and the interfaces and dependencies with other systems. The framework also notes that the inventory should contain information used to measure the progress and value of the investments, such as benefits to the mission, schedule, risk assessments, and performance metrics. Without a complete inventory of IT information, an organization cannot develop an adequate investment control process, and consequently, will lack the foundation for demonstrating the impact of alternative investment strategies and funding levels for the agency's inventory of information resources.

Although FDA reported spending approximately $439 million for IT investments in fiscal year 2011, the agency does not have a comprehensive list of IT systems identifying and providing key information about the systems that it currently uses or is developing. In response to our request for an inventory of systems, FDA officials pointed to two sources that partly identified key elements of the agency's systems:

- information contained in key budget and planning documents it prepares annually for submission to OMB, and

- a list of 21 mission-critical systems[21] and modernization initiatives (see app. III for the list of 21 systems and modernization initiatives).

However, while these sources identified certain key investments with varying levels of detail as to cost, purpose, and status, the CIO and agency officials responsible for developing an inventory acknowledged that the information was not comprehensive and lacked critical details about systems that would be essential to effectively managing the

---

[21]FDA defines its mission-critical systems as applications needed to be operational in the event of a government shutdown.

agency's IT investments.[22] Specifically, OMB requires federal departments and agencies, including the Department of Health and Human Services—of which FDA is a component—to annually provide information related to their IT investment portfolios (called exhibit 53s) and capital asset plans and business cases for major investments (called exhibit 300s). The purpose of the exhibit 53 is to identify all IT investments—both major and nonmajor—and their associated costs for which funding is being sought in a particular fiscal year. The exhibit 300s provide a business case for each major IT investment, and agencies are required to provide information on each major investment's cost, schedule, and performance.[23]

For fiscal year 2011, FDA's exhibit 53 identified development and operations and maintenance costs for 44 IT investments. (See app. IV for a list of the 44 IT investments.) For example, one of the 44 line items in the exhibit 53 identified an investment for FDA's Information and Computing Technologies for the 21st Century (ICT21), with about $68 million in funding for fiscal year 2011. In addition, FDA submitted an exhibit 300 for eight major investments. Among these investments were ICT21 and the Automated Laboratory Management project, which is to facilitate communication between FDA labs by creating an electronic environment based on a standardized format.

However, while these documents contain key IT information, such as costs of the investments, they did not present a comprehensive list of FDA's systems with the detailed information that would be essential to managing the agency's portfolio. For example, the exhibit 53 provides investment cost information for the previous year, current year, and budget year, but does not include any information on the performance of the investments. Further, while exhibit 300s provide information on the

---

[22]In July 2011, FDA's Chief Technology Officer and the former acting CIO said that the agency has lists of IT systems that were used to manage a recently completed data center consolidation, but these were not comprehensive. Further, in February 2012, a senior technical advisor said that FDA has multiple lists of systems, including systems identified in enterprise architecture reports and in capital planning investment documents. However, the official said that these lists require extensive revisions and validation before they are completed.

[23]OMB guidance defines a major information system as one that requires special management attention because of its importance to an agency mission; its high development, operating, or maintenance costs; or its significant role in administration of agency programs, finances, property, or other resources.

major investments, they do not provide comprehensive detailed information on the systems that comprise these investments. For example, exhibit 300s may not include detailed information on the systems' interfaces, dependencies, or performance.

In addition to the OMB budget documents, the agency's list of 21 mission-critical systems and modernization initiatives did not fully identify FDA's IT systems. Agency officials acknowledged that this list was partly derived from a list of enterprisewide systems discussed in our prior (June 2009) report and did not include all systems. For example, while the list did include some of the regulatory systems critical to CFSAN's mission, such as MARCS, the FDA Unified Registration and Listing System, and the Low-Acid Canned Foods system, the list did not include other systems identified by the centers as critical to their missions. Among these, the list did not include information on two of three mission-critical systems belonging to the Center for Drug Evaluation and Research: the Document Archiving, Reporting and Regulatory Tracking System, which tracks drug applications; and the Electronic Drug Registration and Listing System, which automates drug firm registrations and implements unique identifiers for all firms. Further, FDA's list did not include the key regulatory and administrative systems used by CFSAN—the CFSAN Adverse Events Reporting System and the Food Applications Regulatory Management system—both of which were identified on the exhibit 53 to OMB.

According to FDA's CIO, the agency is in the process of reviewing IT projects of over $5 million and identifying potential improvements in its capital planning and investment control process to increase insight into the IT portfolio. However, the CIO and a senior technical advisor could not say when the comprehensive list of systems would be finalized. Until the agency has a comprehensive inventory of its IT assets, it will lack the information needed to ensure that it is identifying the appropriate mix of investments that best meet its needs and priorities. Further, lacking such an inventory, the agency substantially diminishes its ability to provide a full picture of the current state of its investments, its vision of the future, and its plan for getting there.

While FDA Has Taken Steps to Modernize Its IT, Much Work Remains, and It Has Not Implemented Key Management Capabilities

FDA has completed several projects aimed at, among other things, modernizing its IT infrastructure and administrative processes. These projects include a data center migration and consolidation effort and efforts aimed at standardizing data across systems. The agency has also nearly completed one major mission-critical system modernization project that provides capabilities supporting its regulatory mission. Nevertheless, much work remains on FDA's largest mission-critical system modernization project, MARCS, and a lack of adequate planning, among other things, makes it uncertain when or if it will meet its goals of replacing eight key legacy systems and providing needed functionality. In addition, FDA has not yet fully implemented key IT management capabilities to guide and support its modernization effort, such as IT strategic planning, enterprise architecture development and implementation, and IT human capital planning.

Data Center Modernization Effort Is Complete, and One Regulatory Modernization Effort Is Nearly Complete

FDA has completed a major effort to modernize its IT operations and infrastructure by consolidating its data centers. Specifically, the ICT21 data center modernization and migration effort replaced the agency's aging data center infrastructure with modern equipment and consolidated its data centers. The effort began in 2008 and was completed in 2011. According to FDA, this effort provided the foundation for modern, networked information and shared data resources and positioned the agency to tackle the challenges of building the next generation of application systems and software tools. FDA officials further noted that the new data centers provide users with greater access to information, having decreased unscheduled system downtime, and that the centers have formalized and standardized the agency's development, test, and production environments to improve operations.

FDA has also nearly completed one of its major enterprisewide mission-critical systems modernization efforts—Medwatch Plus—which is estimated to cost about $56 million. Medwatch Plus is to provide a reporting portal for the public to submit adverse event reports as well as the capability to create reports to inform the public of safety problems. FDA receives more than 600,000 voluntary postmarketing adverse event reports annually from manufacturers, health care professionals, and consumers for all FDA-regulated products, many of which are submitted as paper reports. According to the agency, the portal provides a user-friendly electronic submission capability, encouraging the reporting of information in a quality and uniform manner. In May 2010, FDA reported that the agency had deployed the Electronic Safety Reporting Portal.[24] This website can be used to report safety problems related to foods, including animal feed and animal drugs, as well as adverse events occurring on human gene transfer trials. According to officials, the project was in operations and maintenance, and the agency's project documentation reported that the project will be enhanced to reflect recent legislation.[25]

Another part of the Medwatch Plus project, the FDA Adverse Event Reporting System is to provide tools for the analysis of adverse events and safety report information. According to FDA, the system will enable the agency to improve the timeliness, accuracy, and usability of its product safety surveillance data by significantly reducing delays and errors associated with manual data entry and coding of paper reports. The system is initially being developed for the analysis of drug and biologic products. FDA estimates that the FDA Adverse Event Reporting System will be deployed in 2012.

Considerable Work Remains on MARCS

While FDA has made important progress toward completing ICT21 and Medwatch Plus, considerable work remains to complete the MARCS program. Initiated in 2002, the program is one of the agency's largest and costliest system efforts, receiving $37 million of FDA's 2011 modernization and operations funding and having a total estimated cost of $280 million.

The need for MARCS arose from problems experienced with FDA's critical compliance systems, such as OASIS. According to the Program Manager, these and other ORA systems were developed in a stove-piped manner, and thus did not easily interface with other FDA systems in place or being developed. Specifically, the Program Manager noted that, while it is not impossible, it is expensive and difficult to develop these interfaces. As a result, FDA employees did not have immediate access to needed

---

[24]In May 2010 when the agency deployed the portal, this project was part of the overall larger IT investment Medwatch Plus; since this time the agency has separated the project from Medwatch Plus and as such the portal is called Medwatch Plus-Electronic Safety Reporting Portal.

[25]FDA Food Safety Modernization Act, Pub. L. No. 111-353, Jan. 4, 2011.

information and often had to make time-consuming efforts to locate the information manually or in other systems.

The MARCS program is intended to support ORA's critical work of safeguarding food, drugs, medical devices, biologics, and veterinary products that the agency regulates. By enhancing existing applications and developing new systems, it is to provide information to headquarters and field users to perform inspections, compliance activities, and laboratory operations. Specifically, it is to automate the workflow and help track and manage information about firm compliance with FDA's regulations. In addition, the program is also intended to be used by other federal, state, and industry users to help support FDA's public health mission. For example, the program is expected to provide improvements in interfacing and exchanging data with U.S. Customs and Border Protection to inspect products imported into the United States. Further, the program is intended to eliminate FDA's existing stove-piped databases to provide automated data and sharing among domestic and foreign inspections. In this regard, FDA plans to update and replace eight key ORA systems that facilitate FDA's compliance activities.

However, despite its importance to FDA's overall modernization efforts, much of the planned functionality has not been delivered, and FDA has yet to retire the legacy systems MARCS was intended to replace. A series of rebaselines and changes to accommodate short-term needs resulted in repeated shifts in the approach and revisions to the target dates for completing the program:

- Since 2002, when the program was initiated, requirements were changed and broadened to include the replacement of six additional legacy systems from the two originally planned.

- In 2005, development was put on hold, and efforts and funding were redirected toward FDA's data center modernization effort and toward providing web-enabled versions of the two original legacy systems, OASIS and FACTS.[26] The program was rebaselined in 2006, 2007, and 2009 to accommodate additional cost or functionality and the replacement of additional legacy systems. According to FDA, in 2010, the agency updated and revalidated MARCS requirements.

---

[26]FACTS is a central data repository for workload management, sample collections, sample analyses, information about firms regulated by the FDA, and investigative operations.

- In August 2011, FDA again rebaselined the MARCS program estimates to account for new legislative and resulting regulatory requirements based on the FDA Food Safety Modernization Act.[27] It estimated that the total life-cycle cost would be $282.7 million[28] and planned to deploy a significant portion of MARCS and retire its legacy systems by July 2014. (For a history of MARCS see app. V.)

Nonetheless, as of February 2012, FDA still had considerable work to accomplish on MARCS. While the agency deployed a tool—the Predictive Risk-based Evaluation for Dynamic Import Compliance Targeting (PREDICT)—to improve the efficiency of the inspection process through targeting high-risk imports, FDA had not yet been able to retire any of the eight legacy systems MARCS was intended to replace. Further, of the approximately 30 planned service components,[29] or major business processes, of the program, only 8 were in the implementation or operations and maintenance phases,[30] while the remaining 22 were in earlier phases, such as requirements analysis. Of these 22, FDA had yet to begin work on 12 components.

Figure 3 shows the life-cycle phases[31] of the program's service components as provided by FDA.

---

[27]Pub. L. No. 111-353.

[28]MARCS life-cycle costs of $282.7 million include FDA's August 2011 rebaseline request for additional funding required to meet the changes for the FDA Food Safety Modernization Act. These funds were not previously included in the fiscal year 2012 OMB exhibit 300.

[29]While FDA noted that there are 37 components, for the purpose of reporting status, the agency grouped 6 components into the Field Work Manager component and 3 into Work Assignment and Accomplishment Management Services, resulting in 30 total components.

[30]According to MARCS users, the six components have improved import entry reviewers' efficiency. For example, PREDICT and MARCS Entry Review (one part of MARCS Entry Manager), were deployed to all 16 import districts by the end of December 2011 and have provided automated look-ups. Specifically, an entry reviewer at the Port of Baltimore said that the automated look-up of data from FDA's low-acid canned foods database, lab data, and medical device approvals reduces the time spent reviewing import entries.

[31]FDA follows HHS's Enterprise Performance Life Cycle Framework, in which projects pass through 10 life-cycle phases: initiation, concept, planning, requirements analysis, design, development, test, implementation, operations and maintenance, and disposition.

Figure 3: MARCS Components by Life-Cycle Phase

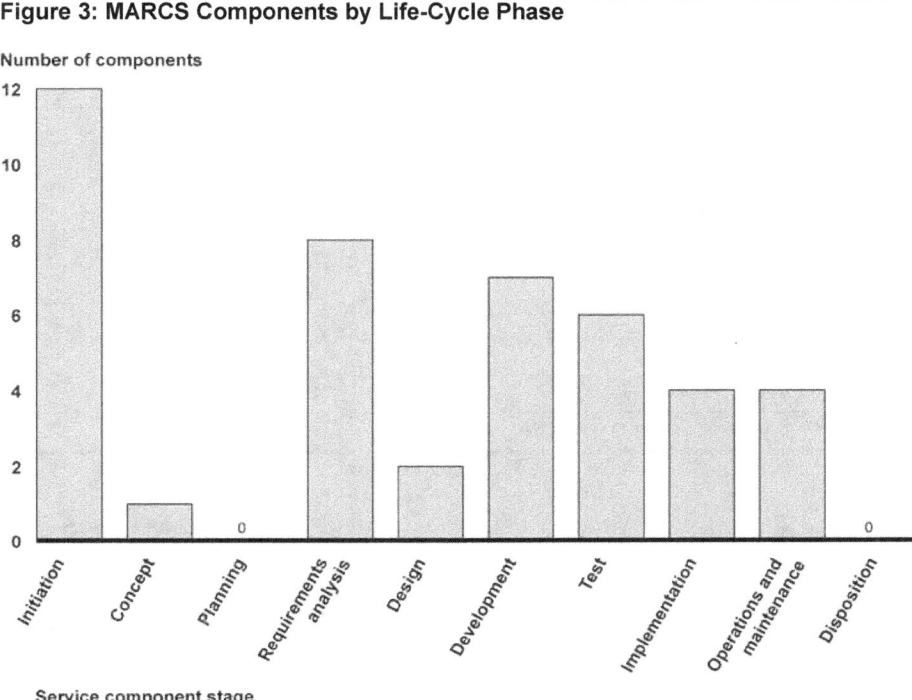

Number of components

Service component stage

Source: GAO analysis of FDA data.

Note: Service components do not sum to 30 because several components have mixed life cycles and are accounted for more than once. FDA stated that it is changing its development approach to MARCS which will require a different way of measuring status in the future.

Among the parts of MARCS that have been completed, FDA incorporated PREDICT—a tool to provide import reviewers with an improved ability to estimate the risk of a product to the public. According to the agency, PREDICT automatically flags potentially risky shipments, such as raw seafood, and gives lower-risk scores to more innocuous materials, which can then be cleared through FDA inspection rapidly. This allows FDA inspectors to spend their time looking at the highest-risk items. It also means that carefully labeled products with good histories will be held up for shorter periods. FDA deployment of PREDICT to all ports was completed by the end of December 2011.

Table 1 provides details on the change in planned retirement dates of legacy systems over time.

Table 1: Planned System Retirement Dates

System	Retirement date as of April 2008 Exhibit 300	Retirement date as of August 2011 Roadmap
Operational Administrative System for Import Support (OASIS)	September 2010	July 2014
Field Accomplishments and Compliance Tracking System (FACTS)	September 2011	July 2014
Electronic State Access to FACTS	September 2012	March 2014
Turbo EIR	September 2008	June 2013
Recall Enterprise System	September 2009	November 2013
Prior Notice System Interface	September 2012	September 2013
Compliance Management System	Not specified	December 2013
Compliance Status Information System	Not specified	July 2014

Source: FDA data.

FDA Has Not Developed an Integrated Master Schedule for MARCS to Effectively Gauge Progress

One critical management tool to effectively determine work remaining of complex systems that involve the integration of a number of components is having a reliable IMS that is used to monitor all of the program's work activities, how long the activities will take, and how the activities are related to one another.[32] The IMS is a top-level schedule that is linked to lower-level schedules that define all of the tasks necessary to complete the project, including work to be performed both by the government and contractors, and that includes all tasks for the life cycle of the project. As such, the IMS provides both a roadmap for systematic execution of a program, and a means by which to gauge progress. It is a critical tool for determining what work remains and the expected cost to complete it and for identifying and addressing potential problems.

While the Program Manger provided a fiscal year 2011 schedule and multiple 2012 subproject schedules, these documents lacked key information that is required in an IMS. Specifically, the fiscal year 2011 schedule does not identify all current and future tasks for the program, and does not reflect the work to be performed by the government as well as the contractor. The schedule reflects activities through fiscal year 2012, but lacks key information on the program's milestones and schedules for the rest of the project, which runs beyond fiscal year

---

[32]GAO, *GAO Cost Estimating and Assessment Guide: Best Practices for Developing and Managing Capital Program Costs*, GAO-09-3SP (March 2009).

2014.[33] Consequently, FDA is only projecting work through the current fiscal year, which does not identify the full scope of the project. Further, the schedule is based on tasks and lower-level schedules of the integration contractor and does not include tasks to be performed by the government. As a result, it does not have the key capability to provide a summary of progress on all lower-level tasks or of the effects of changes to lower-level schedules and tasks on the overall project. Thus, it cannot be used to gauge progress on the entire project and evaluate the effect of changes to individual tasks on the project as a whole.

Instead of an IMS, the MARCS contractor program manager noted that FDA and the contractor are using separate schedules to manage the work and are coordinating their schedules at biweekly meetings. FDA officials also told us that they had not developed a detailed schedule of future tasks because there are many unknowns, including funding availability and changes to functionality needed as a result of legislation such as the FDA Food Safety Modernization Act. While our cost estimating guide says that a comprehensive schedule should reflect all activities for a project, it recognizes that there can be uncertainties and unknown factors in schedule estimates due to, among other things, limited data.[34] In response to such uncertainties and unknowns, the guidance discusses the need to perform a schedule risk analysis to determine the level of uncertainty and to help identify and mitigate the risks.

Although FDA updated and revalidated MARCS requirements in 2010, the agency is in the process of determining if the program meets the agency's business needs. The CIO noted that the program's requirements may be outdated and that as part of his reevaluation of FDA's modernization efforts, the agency intends to refocus and scope down the project. Moreover, he stated that he needs to reassess when or whether MARCS will replace and retire the legacy systems. Until this assessment is complete, it is uncertain how or when much of the intended functionality and improvements associated with MARCS will be delivered. Further, without an IMS to coordinate the efforts associated with a

---

[33]FDA has a roadmap for MARCS that provides a high-level plan for 2011 through 2014 of the service components, but it does not specify all of the program's work activities, their sequencing, or required resources.

[34]GAO-09-3SP.

rescoped version of the program, FDA increases the risk that it will be unable to successfully execute all activities needed to complete the program, resulting in additional delays in delivering improved functionality and retiring legacy systems.

FDA Has Not Fully Established Key IT Management Capabilities Needed to Guide Its Modernization Efforts

An agency's chance of success in modernizing its IT systems, particularly for large and costly programs such as MARCS, is improved if it institutes key IT management capabilities. However, FDA has not fully established key IT management capabilities including IT strategic planning, enterprise architecture, and IT human capital planning. As the agency undertakes its modernization initiatives, an IT strategic plan should serve as the agency's vision or roadmap and help align its information resources with its business strategies and investment decisions. Further, an enterprise architecture can provide a blueprint for the modernization effort by defining models that describe how an organization operates today (the "as-is" state), and how it intends to operate in the future (the "to-be" state), along with a plan for transitioning to the future state. In addition, strategic human capital planning is essential to ensuring that an organization has the right number of people with the right mix of knowledge and skills to achieve current and future program results. Until FDA establishes these capabilities, successful completion of its modernization efforts is in jeopardy.

FDA Does Not Have an Actionable IT Strategic Plan to Guide Its Modernization Efforts

As we have previously reported, IT strategic plans serve as an agency's vision or roadmap and help align its information resources with its business strategies and investment decisions.[35] Further, such a plan is an important asset to document the agency's vision for the future in key areas of IT management, including enterprise architecture development and human capital planning. Among other things, the plan might include the mission of the agency, key business processes, IT challenges, and guiding principles. Further, a strategic plan is important to enable an agency to consider the resources, including human, infrastructure, and funding, that are needed to manage, support, and pay for projects. For example, a strategic plan that identifies what an agency intends to accomplish during a given period helps ensure that the necessary infrastructure is put in place for new or improved capabilities. In addition, a strategic plan that identifies interdependencies within and across

---

[35]GAO-09-523.

individual IT systems modernization projects helps ensure that the interdependencies are understood and managed, so that projects—and thus system solutions—are effectively integrated.

FDA does not have an actionable[36] IT strategic plan that identifies specific goals and corresponding tasks to guide its overall modernization efforts, although our June 2009 report recommended that it develop one. While the agency drafted an IT strategic plan in May 2010, this plan has not been completed or approved by agency executives. A senior technical advisor stated that the plan was not sufficiently detailed or actionable and the agency is revising and updating the plan. However, the official was unable to provide details on when it would be finalized or available for review. In January 2012, FDA's CIO stated that the agency was undertaking an extensive effort to collect feedback to inform a strategic direction.

Our prior report recommended that FDA develop an IT strategic plan that includes results-oriented goals, strategies, milestones, and performance measures and use this plan to guide and coordinate its modernization projects and activities.[37] Until the agency implements this recommendation, FDA will lack a comprehensive picture of the goals of its efforts and the strategies that will be used to meet them. Consequently, FDA risks proceeding with IT modernization efforts that are not well planned and coordinated, that are not sufficiently aligned with the agency's strategic goals, and that include dependent projects that are not synchronized.

FDA's Enterprise Architecture Remains Incomplete

An agency's enterprise architecture describes both its business operations and the technology it uses to carry out those operations. It is a blueprint for organizational change defined in models that describe (in both business and technology terms) how an entity operates today and how it intends to operate in the future; it also includes a plan for transitioning to this future state. According to our enterprise architecture management maturity framework, an organization should develop a documented enterprise architecture program management plan,

---

[36]According to FDA, the agency's draft IT strategic plan was not actionable because it only contained high-level milestones and did not provide component tasks, schedules, and dates needed to execute and track progress toward its modernization efforts.

[37]GAO-09-523.

describing in detail the steps to be taken and tasks to be performed in managing the enterprise architecture program, including a detailed work breakdown and estimates for funding and staffing.[38] When planning IT modernization, a to-be enterprise architecture provides a view of what is planned for the agency's performance, business, data, services, technology, and security architectures, and is supplemented with a plan for transitioning from the as-is to the to-be state. This is critical in order to coordinate the concurrent development of IT systems in a manner that increases the likelihood that systems will be able to interoperate and that they will be able to use the IT infrastructure that is planned going forward. In addition, organizations can develop an architecture in segments—referred to as a segment architecture—that correspond to business areas or domains in order to divide the development process into manageable sections. According to the Federal Enterprise Architecture Practice Guidance, prioritizing segments should precede building them, and developing the segment architecture should take place before an agency executes its IT projects for a segment.[39] Attempting to define and build major IT systems without first completing either an enterprisewide architecture or, where appropriate, the relevant segment architectures, is risky.

We reported in 2009 that FDA had made mixed progress in establishing its enterprise architecture and that the agency did not yet have an architecture that could be used to efficiently and effectively guide its modernization efforts. Since then, the agency's enterprise architecture has remained incomplete.

Specifically, the agency has developed a draft enterprise architecture management plan; however, according to FDA's Chief Enterprise Architect, the plan needs to be rewritten to reflect recent guidance from OMB and HHS, as well as the new CIO's vision. In addition, the plan does not address all the elements called for by GAO's enterprise architecture management maturity framework, such as identifying needed funding and staff resources. The Chief Enterprise Architect estimated that the revised

---

[38]GAO, *Organizational Transformation: A Framework for Assessing and Improving Enterprise Architecture Management,* Version 2.0, GAO-10-846G (Washington, D.C.: August 2010).

[39]OMB, Federal Enterprise Architecture Practice Guidance (November, 2007).

enterprise architecture management plan would be completed in April 2012.

Further, FDA has not completed its as-is architecture, particularly in describing its current environment in terms of technology, performance, and security; nor has FDA completed its to-be architecture by describing, for example, desired end-to-end business information flows, or developed an enterprise architecture transition plan. FDA has developed architecture products that describe aspects of the as-is enterprise architecture in terms of business processes, information, and IT systems. For example, it has drafted a graphical high-level view of FDA's business process hierarchy, which shows the core mission processes, mission-enabling processes, and IT capabilities; and has produced a report of current FDA information exchange packages and identified data standards. However, FDA's architecture products do not adequately describe its as-is environment in terms of technology, performance, and security. For example,

- although FDA has defined a high-level technical standards review process and identified certain as-is technology products, it has not described enterprise-level as-is technology infrastructure assets, such as common application servers and communications networks that currently support enterprise application systems and services; and

- FDA's architecture products do not describe enterprise-level as-is performance issues and security concerns.

These descriptions are important since they provide a basis for making decisions on enterprise investments and developing an enterprise transition roadmap.

FDA has developed an initial draft of its target enterprise architecture that describes aspects of its to-be environment. The target enterprise architecture is defined in terms of business needs, information, services, technology, and security. For example, it identifies business functions (e.g., facility inspection) performed by FDA, the classes of data (e.g., facility inspection data) used by the business functions (e.g., product review and approval), and the types of technology infrastructure (e.g., enterprise service bus) used across FDA. The target enterprise architecture also includes a technical reference architecture diagram that identifies logical groupings of services and a services integration framework.

Nonetheless, the target architecture does not adequately describe FDA's to-be environment. For example, the target architecture does not include to-be end-to-end business information flows that identify the information used by FDA in its business processes, where the information is needed, and how the information is shared to support mission functions. These artifacts are necessary to help FDA identify process gaps and information-sharing requirements among its business functions, data centers, and systems; across business segments; and with external business partners (e.g., life sciences companies and food companies). Moreover, it does not identify enterprise policies for the way information is acquired, accessed, shared, and used within FDA and by its business partners. Further, it does not describe common application components and reusable services expected to be leveraged by all segments and identify as-is cross-agency applications that are expected to be part of the target environment.

In addition, the FDA target architecture does not include performance measures that focus on the long-term performance of the entire agency and performance targets established for all key business processes and agency services. This information is important since it establishes a basis for defining the expected performance of related segments and the technical performance of the supporting application systems and services. Moreover, FDA has not adequately described its to-be environment in terms of technology. For example, although the Chief Enterprise Architect indicated that cloud computing services and solutions would be adopted for sharing information internally and externally, the architecture does not yet provide the timelines for transitioning to cloud computing and identify what databases, services, and platforms are to take advantage of cloud-based services.

Further, FDA has completed only 1 of 12 architecture segments that will make up its enterprise architecture, and continues to conduct modernization and system development efforts for segments it has not completed. Finally, FDA has not developed plans that address the risk of proceeding with modernization projects in the absence of a complete architecture.

We previously recommended that FDA accelerate development of its segment and enterprise architecture, including the as-is and to-be architectures and the associated transition plan.[40] As long as its enterprise architecture and segment architectures lag behind its modernization projects, FDA increases the risk that its modernization projects will not conform to its planned environment and that the IT solutions that it pursues will not be defined, developed, and deployed in a way that promotes sharing and interoperability, maximizes shared reuse, and minimizes overlap and duplication. Finally, without a plan to address risks associated with an incomplete target architecture and transition plan, there is no assurance that appropriate actions will be taken, including risk identification and prioritization, risk response, and risk monitoring and control.

FDA Has Not Planned Adequately for Its IT Human Capital Needs

The success or failure of federal programs, like those of other organizations, depends on having the right number of people with the right mix of knowledge and skills. In our prior work, we have found that strategic human capital management is essential to the success of any organization.[41] Strategic human capital management focuses on two principles that are critical in a modern, results-oriented management environment:

- People are assets whose value can be enhanced through investment.

- An organization's human capital approaches must be aligned to support the mission, vision for the future, core values, goals and objectives, and strategies by which the organization has defined its direction.

In our model of strategic human capital management and our report on principles for strategic workforce planning, we identified principles for managing human capital.[42] In this regard, strategic workforce planning involves determining the critical skills and competencies needed to achieve current and future program results (these should be linked to

---

[40]GAO-09-523.

[41]For example, our prior work has shown negative cost and schedule implications for complex services acquisitions at the Department of Homeland Security that did not have adequate staff. See GAO, *Department of Homeland Security: Better Planning and Assessment Needed to Improve Outcomes for Complex Service Acquisitions*, GAO-08-263 (Washington, D.C.: Apr. 22, 2008).

[42]GAO, *Human Capital: Key Principles for Effective Strategic Workforce Planning*, GAO-04-39 (Washington, D.C.: Dec. 11, 2003).

long-term goals), analyzing the gaps between current skills and future needs, and developing strategies for filling gaps.

However, FDA has not adequately planned for its human capital needs, although our June 2009 report recommended that it do so. Our prior review found that the agency had not inventoried the skills of its IT workforce, determined present or future skills needs, or analyzed gaps. Since our prior review, the agency has made limited progress in assessing its IT human capital needs.

In March 2010, FDA reported the results of its workforce assessment of OIM's Division of Systems. The report documented current workforce characteristics based on a survey of Division of Systems employees and recommended steps for the division to better align its functions and responsibilities with the needs of the centers. However, the survey was limited to only one of OIM's five divisions (Division of Systems Management), and did not consider work performed by contractors.[43] Further, while the assessment identified staff concerns with their ability to perform current and future tasks, it only provided a snapshot of current capabilities, and did not include an estimate of skills and resources needed to perform future work or an assessment of whether the skills and abilities of the current workforce are sufficient to meet future needs.

In August 2011, the agency reported on a more comprehensive study of IT staff skills and resource allocations. This study was also, in part, based on a survey of OIM's IT staff, and it included all five of OIM's divisions. However, the study was focused on current workload information and included staff's self-reported estimates of calendar year 2010 hours and a prediction of 2011 hours for IT functional areas. The study was not based on an assessment of needs to achieve future IT plans. Further, the study did not include a gap analysis based on future IT plans.

Thus, FDA has yet to conduct a full assessment of future needs, and develop a plan to address them. When asked about additional plans to address the gaps in its IT human capital planning, the Acting Chief Operating Officer said that further IT human capital assessments and

[43]The other four divisions were not included in the survey, specifically, the Division of Business Partnership and Support, Division of Infrastructure Operations, Division of CIO Support, and Division of Technology.

planning would not occur until the new CIO could be briefed on the assessments that have been performed to date and the findings.

The CIO stated that workforce modernization is one of the most critical needs for FDA to effectively meet its future IT goals. According to the CIO, each of FDA's operating divisions was in the process of identifying the skill sets needed to replace OIM staff that departed the agency. The CIO cited shortages in staff that have experience building clinical data warehouses—a critical agency need. The CIO also stated that the agency's IT staff skills have been limited by inadequate training and added that FDA plans to fill the agency's human capital gaps through obtaining external expertise and internal development. However, without a human capital plan to guide these efforts, FDA risks not obtaining the right number of people with the right mix of skills to meet its goals.

Moreover, beyond deficiencies in its staff skill sets and inadequate training, the agency's ability to manage IT has also been hindered by changes in leadership. Since 2008, the agency has had five CIOs, potentially hampering its ability to plan and effectively implement a long-range IT strategy. For example, the agency had two acting CIOs during 2011, with a permanent CIO only being selected recently (in October 2011). According to the former Acting CIO, FDA filled positions with acting officials in order to address specific goals. For example, in March 2011, he was moved from his position as OIM Director of IT Infrastructure to the acting CIO position because FDA considered his expertise essential to completing the data center consolidation effort. However, without a CIO with a broad view of IT strategic goals, the agency was unable to focus on its longer-term objectives. Further, this has led to planning delays in key areas such as IT strategic planning, enterprise architecture development, and human capital management. In September 2011, for example, the agency's Chief Operating Officer said that IT human capital plans were on hold until the new CIO was in place. We noted previously that one element that influences the likely success of an agency CIO is the length of time the individual in the position has to implement change. For example, our prior work has noted that it can take 5 to 7 years to fully implement major change initiatives in large public and private sector organizations and to transform related cultures in a sustainable manner.

In our previous review of FDA's modernization efforts, we recommended that the agency develop a human capital plan that includes an assessment of skills, determines needs, and analyzes gaps.[44] Until the agency does so and maintains stable leadership to guide its efforts, the agency risks not having adequate management and staff in key areas necessary to effectively manage its IT modernization efforts.

FDA Has Made Mixed Progress in More Effectively Sharing and Integrating Data

Data sharing is critical for FDA to effectively carry out its mission. As previously noted, the agency needs timely access to data to be able to support its product review and approval process, its inspection of imports and manufacturing facilities, and its postmarket surveillance activities. Further, the agency needs to collect data from and share them with a wide array of partners, including public health organizations, importers, and other federal entities, as well as the general public. Specifically, it needs standardized data to effectively compare information of thousands of drug studies and clinical trials. Both we and the HHS Inspector General have previously identified challenges, such as inconsistent naming conventions, in the agency's ability to share information, both internally and with external partners.[45]

FDA has taken some steps to improve its sharing of data, but much more remains to be done. Specifically, the agency has several initiatives under way to more effectively share its data, including adopting an enterprisewide standard for formatting data, and several projects aimed at enhancing its ability to share data, both internally and with external partners. However, these projects have made mixed progress, and more significant work remains for FDA to fully implement standardized data sharing across the agency.

---

[44]GAO-09-523.

[45]See, for example, GAO, *Food and Drug Administration: Response to Heparin Contamination Helped Protect Public Health; Controls That Were Needed for Working with External Entities Were Recently Added*, GAO-11-95 (Washington, D.C.: Oct. 29, 2010); *Drug Safety: FDA Has Begun Efforts to Enhance Postmarket Safety, but Additional Actions Are Needed*, GAO-10-68 (Washington, D.C.: Nov. 9, 2009); GAO-10-699T; HHS Office of Inspector General, *Challenges to FDA's Ability to Monitor and Inspect Foreign Clinical Trials*, OEI-01-08-00510 (June 2010); HHS Office of Inspector General, *FDA's Food Facility Registry*, OEI-02-08-00060 (December 2009); and HHS Office of Inspector General, *Adverse Event Reporting for Medical Devices*, OEI-01-08-00110 (October 2009).

FDA Has Adopted an Enterprisewide Standard to Facilitate Data Sharing and Analysis

Data standardization includes ensuring that information is submitted and stored in a consistent format using consistent terminology. Developing systems based on the use and enforcement of data standards helps ensure that information collected is complete and consistent and that users of the data exchanged have a common understanding. The ultimate benefit of standardizing data is to make it easier to collect, compare, maintain, and analyze.

FDA has made progress in one significant initiative aimed at achieving more effective sharing of data: its adoption of an enterprisewide data standard that can be applied to food, drugs, and medical devices. Specifically, it has adopted an HL7 international health care informatics interoperability standard as its enterprisewide data model. The standard that the agency has adopted—Reference Information Model, HL7 version 3[46]—provides a set of rules that allow information to be shared and processed in a uniform and consistent manner. For example, it specifies formats for presenting the names of firms or products, descriptions of disease symptoms, or the gender of a patient (e.g., "M" or "Male"). This standardization of data formats should help ensure consistency in how information on products is submitted to FDA; it also should facilitate analysis of the data by making it easier to compare information across products or to identify patterns in large numbers of data (i.e., data mining). As such, it should provide the foundations for FDA's efforts to standardize data enterprisewide.

FDA is applying this standard to multiple categories of products, including food, drugs, and medical devices, in order to facilitate the input, reading, and comparison of information on applicable products submitted to the agency for approval. For example, it has established an Electronic Submissions Gateway, which provides a virtual "mailbox" that accepts submissions of drug studies and other information. In addition, the gateway has an HL7 screening capability that reviews submissions to ensure that they meet FDA's data standards. This could facilitate the drug companies submitting data to ensure the information is consistent with the required standard.

---

[46]This standard provides a number of benefits: it is accredited by the American National Standards Institute; incorporates current IT standards for system development, use cases, and data methodology; and, according to the Healthcare Information Technology Standards Panel, complies with Health Insurance Portability and Accountability Act standards.

However, according to the agency, currently only about 60 percent[47] of clinical trial data is being submitted electronically, with the remainder being submitted on paper. The amount of paper submissions hinders the agency's development and implementation of standardized data for electronic submission. The adoption of electronic submission continues to be limited because its use is voluntary, in that submitters can choose to use the older paper format that does not conform to the data standards. FDA officials said they are promoting electronic submission of applications and reports by educating submitters on the benefits of electronic submissions.

In addition to its adoption of an enterprisewide data standard, FDA has developed an approach to standardizing firm registration data that it receives in a nonstandard format.[48] While this provides the agency with consistency in data on firms, agency officials acknowledged that there is considerable work remaining to implement data standardization across the agency. Moreover, these officials stated that acquiring the staff with needed expertise in areas such as data modeling remains a challenge. For example, FDA is developing a wide array of standards in collaboration with industry representatives to evaluate and reach agreement on how these standards will be implemented and adopted.

Data-Sharing Projects Have Made Mixed Progress

In addition to its adoption of the HL7 data standard, FDA has several initiatives that are intended to enhance the sharing of data throughout the agency. Of four such initiatives, two are in the mixed phase of development,[49] one is in an early stage of development, and the other is on hold pending a reevaluation. Table 2 shows the progress these projects have made since 2009.

---

[47]Booz Allen Hamilton, *FDA Evaluations and Studies of New Drug Review Programs Under PDUFA IV for the FDA, Assessment of the Impact of the Electronic Submission and Review Environment on the Efficiency and Effectiveness of the Review of Human Drugs - Final Report* (Sept. 9, 2011).

[48]The Firms Master List Services standardizes and validates the facility name and address data received from imports, registration and listing systems, and inspections. The Firms Master List Services is used by MARCS and Automated Laboratory Management.

[49]A mixed life-cycle investment means an investment having both modernization/enhancement and maintenance components. For example, a portion of the system is completed and in maintenance but other components are still under development and being released in phases.

GAO-12-346 FDA Information Technology

Table 2: Status of FDA Data-Sharing Projects

Project	Intended functions and services	2009 Status	2012 Status
Automated Laboratory Management	Standardize the data exchanges and facilitate communication between labs by creating an electronic environment based on a standardized format.	Planning	Mixed
Harmonized Inventory	Standardize about 20 IT systems, such as inspections and compliance systems, to help ensure data consistency and accuracy and avoid duplicate information. Integrate standardized business processes and data elements throughout FDA.	Mixed	Mixed
Regulated Product Submission	International effort to develop a single standard for electronic submission of information on regulated products, including food additives, medical devices, and veterinary products to regulatory authorities, such as FDA and corresponding agencies in other nations.	Planning	Requirements development
Janus	Create an informatics system that can rapidly provide FDA staff with the ability to retrieve and analyze data about regulated products using structured scientific data.	Planning	On hold

Source: GAO analysis of FDA data.

Specifically, FDA has two initiatives in the mixed development stage:

• Automated Laboratory Management: This initiative encompasses several projects focused on improving the efficiency of the staff at ORA laboratories, the quality and quantity of the information the labs provide, and the ability of the office to share and assess information within its own, third-party, and other public health labs. The initiative is intended to provide capabilities for (1) sharing information during food and biological emergencies; (2) greater automation of laboratories, including automated collection and processing of analytical data; and (3) a structured and well defined approach to improving and maintaining quality. Ultimately, the goal of the initiative is to expand ORA's scientific capabilities and improve FDA's ability to share results with federal, state, local, and international officials and agencies, facilitating improved management of risks associated with FDA-regulated products. FDA had deployed, in 2011, one of three[50]

---

[50] According to FDA, Automated Laboratory Management consists of three components: the Electronic Laboratory Exchange Network, the Quality Management Information System, and the Laboratory Information Management System.

components—the Electronic Laboratory Exchange Network portion of Automated Laboratory Management that provides information on food hazards and is shared by several government agencies. Another component, the Quality Management Information System, is in the mixed phase of development, and the Laboratory Information Management System is in design. The agency plans to implement this component by December 2013.

- Harmonized Inventory: This agencywide initiative aims to standardize and improve the data quality of firm and product information by standardizing about 20 IT systems that did not have standardized data and processes. The system processes electronic registration and listing submissions from commercial registrants and labelers engaged in FDA-related activities. According to FDA, in October 2011, the agency completed deployment of a data repository module that provides access to registration data since 2009. The compliance module is in the design and development stage and planned to be implemented by October 2012.[51]

However, of the remaining two data-sharing initiatives, one is still in early stages, and another has been put on hold pending a reevaluation by the FDA CIO:

- The Regulated Product Submission project is part of an international effort to develop a single standard, using HL7 standards, for electronic submission of information on regulated products, including food additives, medical devices, and veterinary products to regulatory authorities in FDA and others, including international agencies. As of 2011, requirements were still being developed for this project.

- Janus was intended to provide FDA with a comprehensive clinical-trial and population-health-data warehouse and analytical tools to enable reviewers to search, model, and analyze data, improving FDA's management of structured scientific data. However, since 2009, this project has only progressed from the planning to the requirements phase. According to the CIO, the project's requirements became too extensive and limited progress was being made in developing the data warehouse. The CIO further noted that FDA did not have the needed expertise for a project this size and scope, and further work

---

[51]FDA Project Dashboard as of December 1, 2011.

has been stopped pending reevaluation. Further, the CIO said that when the project is restarted, the agency will use an Agile[52] software development approach to provide added capabilities incrementally over shorter timeframes to more effectively manage the project.

FDA Has Not Adequately Assessed Data-Sharing Opportunities within the Center for Food Safety and Applied Nutrition

OMB and the Federal CIO Council guidance state that agencies should analyze their business and information environments to determine information-sharing requirements and identify improvement opportunities.[53] The agency's enterprise architecture should demonstrate information sharing within the agency and other government agencies. Further, OMB guidance requires federal agencies to analyze the information used in their business process to indicate where the information is needed and how it is shared to support mission functions. Documenting information flows is an initial step in developing systems and databases that are organized efficiently, are easier to maintain, and meet the user's needs.

However, we have previously identified deficiencies in CFSAN's ability to effectively share information, such as information on recalls of contaminated foods.[54] In particular, CFSAN has 21 different databases and systems that contain information critical to its mission. (See app. VI for details on the center's systems.) These databases and systems contain information on adverse events; seafood inspection; milk shippers; shellfish shippers; retail food safety inspections; toxicological effects of food ingredients and additives; and FDA research on food, animal feed, veterinary medicine, and cosmetics, among others.

The center now has data-sharing initiatives under way, but it has not performed a comprehensive review to identify opportunities for improved data sharing within the center. CFSAN has conducted some work to

---

[52]Agile software development emphasizes selected values, such as the following: the highest priority is to satisfy customers through early and continuous delivery of valuable software; delivering working software frequently, from a couple of weeks to a couple of months; and that working software is the primary measure of progress. For more information on Agile development, see http://www.agilealliance.org.

[53]OMB, *Improving Agency Performance Using Information and Information Technology: Enterprise Architecture Assessment Framework*, Version 3.1 (June 2009), and Federal CIO Council, *Federal Segment Architecture Methodology (FSAM)*, Version 1.0 (Dec. 8, 2008).

[54]GAO-08-597, GAO-09-258, and GAO-10-699T.

improve the sharing of data among these systems and databases. For example, according to the agency, the center has plans for a web-based application designed to standardize vocabularies across systems and enable enterprisewide searching of its disparate data collections.

Nonetheless, the center has not comprehensively assessed its information-sharing needs and capabilities to identify further opportunities for data sharing and system integration. This would examine how information moves between business processes and identify efficiencies that could be gained by grouping related information into corresponding databases. Instead, the center has identified opportunities for data sharing on an ad hoc basis, relying primarily on the expertise of its staff. CFSAN officials acknowledged that integration among its databases could be improved to more effectively share data and streamline processes. For example, certain firms are currently required to access two separate databases to complete the low-acid canned foods registration process. Further, officials noted that the center's systems were generally created in response to a specific need or legislation and are thus stove-piped, with little overlap of information. However, without identifying opportunities for greater and more efficient information sharing, FDA and CFSAN face a risk of continuing to maintain an IT environment that requires greater effort to access needed information.

Conclusions

While FDA has taken several important steps toward modernizing its IT environment, much remains to be done, and these efforts have not been guided by key foundational IT management practices, which expose them to significant risk. Specifically, because FDA does not have a comprehensive list of its systems, it cannot ensure that it is investing in the mix of projects that will best support its mission and that it is managing them appropriately. Further, while FDA has taken foundational steps for IT modernization—including consolidating and updating its data centers and completing modernization projects for some IT systems—FDA has experienced ongoing delays and changes of direction to the MARCS program, one of its largest systems modernization efforts. This state of flux is exacerbated by the lack of an IMS for the program, resulting in uncertainty about when, or if, the planned functionality will be delivered and the ORA legacy systems retired. Compounding these concerns, FDA has yet to establish key IT planning and management disciplines that remain essential for carrying out a successful modernization effort. Without an actionable IT strategic plan, a complete enterprise architecture, and attention to its IT human capital needs, FDA will continue to be challenged in completing its modernization efforts. If implemented, our previous recommendations to establish these IT capabilities could help FDA successfully carry out these efforts. Finally, while FDA has taken important steps to improve its sharing of mission-critical data, until CFSAN conducts a full assessment of its data-sharing needs it may be missing opportunities for increased efficiencies and a reduction in duplication and unnecessary effort. While the agency's new CIO is reassessing several aspects of FDA's modernization program, it remains crucial that any future efforts are guided by rigorous and disciplined planning and management.

Recommendations for Executive Action

To help ensure the success of FDA's modernization efforts, we are recommending that the Commissioner of FDA direct the CIO to take the following four actions:

- Take immediate steps to identify all of FDA's IT systems and develop an inventory that includes information describing each system, such as costs, system function or purpose, and status information, and incorporate use of the system portfolio into the agency's IT investment management process.

- In completing the assessment of MARCS, develop an IMS that

    - identifies which legacy systems will be replaced and when;

    - identifies all current and future tasks to be performed by contractors and FDA; and

    - defines and incorporates information reflecting resources and critical dependencies.

- Monitor progress of MARCS against the IMS.

- Assess information-sharing needs and capabilities of CFSAN to identify potential areas of improvements needed to achieve more efficient information sharing among databases and develop a plan for implementing these improvements.

Agency Comments and Our Evaluation

HHS provided written comments on a draft of this report, signed by the Assistant Secretary for Legislation (the comments are reproduced in app. II). In its comments, the department neither agreed nor disagreed with our recommendations but stated that FDA has taken actions to address many of the issues in our report.

In its comments, HHS stated that FDA's initiative to modernize its IT infrastructure comprises multiple phases. The first phase includes the data center modernization effort, which the department stated has provided FDA with an advanced computing infrastructure and a production data center with a secure computing environment. According to HHS, this infrastructure modernization and consolidation effort serves as the foundation for all other transition activities, and positions FDA to move forward with the second phase: implementing data center operation management and service contract efficiencies while working on modernizing and consolidating software systems with similar business processes and expediting the retirement of legacy systems.

Our report recognizes the progress that FDA has made in modernizing its data center infrastructure, and we agree that this effort is a key component of the agency's overall modernization initiative. However, as we also noted, over the last decade—and concurrent with its data center modernization effort—FDA has spent tens of millions of dollars on software systems modernization projects that were intended to provide updated functionality and enable the retirement of legacy systems. In particular, FDA spent approximately $160 million from fiscal year 2002 to fiscal year 2011 on MARCS, yet it has repeatedly delayed milestones for delivering capabilities and retiring legacy systems. Moreover, this spending on system development and modernization has occurred in the absence of fully implemented IT management capabilities such as an IT strategic plan, a complete enterprise architecture, and a strategic approach to IT human capital, as well as an IMS for MARCS.

HHS also identified several recent efforts that it stated will address issues we raised in our report:

- FDA's senior executive team (which includes the CIO) has committed to governing the agency's IT portfolio. As part of these responsibilities, the team has conducted sessions to identify the top 5 to 10 capabilities that are needed for the agency to meet the challenges of operating in a globalized regulatory environment. Further, to assist in the management of IT investments, FDA's Office of Information Management is in the process of establishing a new Project Management Office to provide effective services aligned with the agency's strategic priorities.

- FDA has initiated several large program or project reviews to identify areas for improvement, potential for streamlining, and projects that should be stopped, continued, or started. Specifically, FDA has evaluated, and halted, the Janus project, and is conducting a detailed review of MARCS. The agency is also revising its draft IT strategic plan and working to define and implement its enterprise architecture.

- FDA is assessing its IT workforce in Office of Information Management divisions to identify skill-set gaps, develop staff training plans, and identify resource needs. The agency stated that it has set aside training dollars and approved staff training plans, but acknowledged that workforce development activities must be a recurring process in order to ensure its skills keep pace with evolving technologies and methodologies. Further, the agency stated that FDA is committed to placing permanent leadership in all remaining acting positions that report directly to the CIO. Specifically, FDA has posted and closed job vacancy announcements for these positions and is evaluating applicants.

As noted in our report, we recognize and support these efforts, many of which have been initiated by the recently hired CIO. The success of these efforts could be enhanced by FDA's full implementation of the recommendations that we have made in this report and in our 2009 report.

Finally, with regard to our recommendation that FDA develop an IT systems inventory that includes information describing each system—such as costs, system function or purpose, and status information—and incorporate use of the system portfolio into the agency's IT investment management process, FDA provided an inventory of systems after we sent the draft report for review. This inventory included information on 282 IT systems, but did not provide all key information, such as cost and status. Moreover, agency officials stated that the inventory had not yet been validated for completeness and accuracy.

HHS also provided technical comments on the report, which we incorporated as appropriate.

As agreed with your office, unless you publicly announce the contents of this report earlier, we plan no further distribution until 30 days from the report date. At that time, we will send copies to the Commissioner of the Food and Drug Administration, appropriate congressional committees, and other interested parties. In addition, the report will be available at no charge on the GAO website at http://www.gao.gov.

If you or your staff have questions on matters discussed in this report, please contact me at (202) 512-6304 or melvinv@gao.gov. Contact points for our Offices of Congressional Relations and Public Affairs may be found on the last page of this report. GAO staff who made contributions to this report are listed in appendix VII.

Sincerely yours,

Valerie C. Melvin

Valerie C. Melvin
Director
Information Management and Technology Resources Issues

Appendix I: Objectives, Scope, and Methodology

Our objectives were to (1) assess the Food and Drug Administration's (FDA) current portfolio of information technology (IT) systems, including the number of systems in use and under development, and their purpose and costs; (2) assess the status and effectiveness of FDA's efforts to modernize the mission-critical systems that support its regulatory programs; and (3) examine the agency's progress in effectively integrating and sharing data among key systems.

To assess FDA's portfolio of IT systems, we reviewed documentation identifying key systems and major modernization initiatives, the Office of Management and Budget's (OMB) exhibit 300s and exhibit 53s, and a list of FDA's mission-critical systems. We evaluated FDA's list of IT systems and modernization initiatives and assessed it against OMB guidance[1] and GAO's IT investment management framework.[2] We reviewed the agency's budget submissions and the investments listed for fiscal year 2011 exhibits 53 and 300 and compared them to other agency documentation providing systems' descriptions. We interviewed agency officials responsible for developing a portfolio of IT systems and the Chief Information Officer (CIO) to assess the agency's plans for identifying improvements in its process of identifying and overseeing a comprehensive IT portfolio.

To assess the status and effectiveness of FDA's efforts to modernize mission-critical systems that support its regulatory program, we reviewed the Department of Health and Human Services' (HHS) Enterprise Performance Life Cycle Framework,[3] FDA's Science Board study, and GAO and other reports discussing previously identified shortfalls in the agency's systems used to support regulatory programs. We assessed the status of FDA's modernization projects by evaluating the agency's system specific documentation, including project descriptions and contractors' statements of work, and interviewing relevant project managers. We also evaluated the projects by Enterprise Performance Life Cycle stage and

---

[1]OMB, *Management of Federal Information Resources*, Circular No. A-130 (Washington, D.C.: Nov. 28, 2000) and *Planning, Budgeting, Acquisition, and Management of Capital Assets*, Circular No. A-11, Part 7 (Washington, D.C.: July 2003).

[2]GAO, *Information Technology Investment Management: A Framework for Assessing and Improving Process Maturity*, Version 1.1, GAO-04-394G (Washington, D.C.: March 2004).

[3]Department of Health and Human Services, *Enterprise Performance Life Cycle Framework* (Washington, D.C.: September 2011).

data reflected on the agency's federal IT Dashboard. Further, because
Mission Accomplishments and Regulatory Compliance Services
(MARCS) was one of the agency's largest and costliest mission-critical
modernization efforts and was considered essential to the Office of
Regulatory Affairs' (ORA) compliance activities, we evaluated the
project's status and whether the effort is following best practices.
Specifically, we assessed the program's documentation, including agency
plans, schedules, and contractor statements of work, as well as various
components and interviewed relevant project managers and technical
specialists. We compared FDA's schedules with best practices for
developing an integrated master schedule to plan and manage the effort.

We also evaluated FDA's progress in addressing our prior
recommendations[4] related to FDA's implementation of key IT
management practices: IT strategic planning, enterprise architecture, and
IT human capital planning. To do so, we looked at whether policies or
processes were in place for IT investment management, human capital,
and enterprise architecture. We based our analysis on three frameworks:
our IT investment management framework, our framework for strategic
human capital management,[5] and our enterprise architecture
management maturity framework.[6]

- The IT investment management framework provides a rigorous
  standardized tool for evaluating an agency's IT investment
  management processes and a roadmap agencies can use for
  improving their investment management processes.

- The framework for strategic human capital management lays out
  principles for managing human capital. We evaluated FDA's policies
  and procedures against this framework.

- The enterprise architecture management maturity framework
  describes stages of maturity in managing enterprise architecture.

---

[4]See GAO, *Information Technology: FDA Needs to Establish Key Plans and Processes
for Guiding Systems Modernization Efforts*, GAO-09-523 (Washington, DC: June 2, 2009).

[5]GAO, *Human Capital: Key Principles for Effective Strategic Workforce Planning*,
GAO-04-39 (Washington, D.C.: Dec. 11, 2003).

[6]GAO, *Information Technology: A Framework for Assessing and Improving Enterprise
Architecture Management (Version 1.1)*, GAO-03-584G (Washington, D.C.: Apr. 1, 2003).

Each stage includes core elements, which are descriptions of a
practice or condition that is needed for effective enterprise
architecture management. We evaluated FDA's implementation of
four core elements from stage 2 (Creating the Management
Foundation for Enterprise Architecture Development and Use). We did
not perform a complete enterprise architecture management maturity
framework assessment, and we did not audit specific IT projects to
analyze how well the policies and procedures were implemented. To
supplement the framework criteria, we used criteria from the Federal
Enterprise Architecture Practice Guidance issued by OMB[7] and
compared FDA's progress on its architecture with these criteria.

To determine the agency's progress in effectively integrating and sharing
data among key systems, we reviewed project plans, schedules, and
other documents describing FDA's efforts to implement Health Level
Seven (HL7) data standardization for the exchange and analysis of
information. We also assessed the progress of modernization initiatives
aimed at improving standards and data sharing. Specifically we assessed
FDA's modernization initiatives by comparing the Enterprise Performance
Life Cycle stage of the projects from 2009 with the project stages in 2012.

We selected FDA's Center for Food Safety and Applied Nutrition
(CFSAN) to assess sharing across databases supporting FDA's
regulatory mission because of previously identified deficiencies in specific
functions, such as sharing on recalls of contaminated foods.[8] We
analyzed the number of CFSAN databases, their purposes, and
corresponding IT systems used, and assessed the efforts and
methodology used by the center to improve information sharing and

---

[7]OMB, Federal Enterprise Architecture Practice Guidance, (November, 2007).

[8]GAO, Food Labeling: FDA Needs to Better Leverage Resources, Improve Oversight, and
Effectively Use Available Data to Help Consumers Select Healthy Foods, GAO-08-597
(Washington, D.C.: Sept. 9, 2008); Seafood Fraud: FDA Program Changes and Better
Collaboration among Key Federal Agencies Could Improve Detection and Prevention,
GAO-09-258 (Washington, D.C.: Feb. 19, 2009); and Food Safety: FDA Could Strengthen
Oversight of Imported Food by Improving Enforcement and Seeking Additional Authorities,
GAO-10-699T (Washington, D.C.: May 6, 2010).

exchange between databases against OMB and Federal CIO Council
enterprise architecture guidance.[9]

We supplemented our analysis with interviews of the agency's CIO, Chief
Technology Officer, Chief Enterprise Architect, Senior Technical Advisor,
and other relevant IT managers regarding management of FDA's IT
portfolio, the status of and plans to modernize key systems such as
MARCS, shortfalls in mission-related systems, IT strategic and human
capital planning, status of enterprise architecture development, and
efforts to improve interoperability of systems that support FDA's
regulatory mission. In addition, we visited FDA facilities at the Port of
Baltimore in Baltimore, Maryland, to observe a demonstration of new
capabilities to screen imports. We requested and received documentation
from FDA on its agencywide modernization projects, including
descriptions of their purpose and project summary status reports showing
their expected completion dates and other milestones.

We conducted this performance audit primarily at FDA's headquarters in
White Oak, Maryland, from March 2011 to March 2012 in accordance with
generally accepted government auditing standards. Those standards
require that we plan and perform the audit to obtain sufficient, appropriate
evidence to provide a reasonable basis for our findings and conclusions
based on our audit objectives. We believe that the evidence obtained
provides a reasonable basis for our findings and conclusions based on
our audit objectives.

---

[9]OMB, *Improving Agency Performance Using Information and Information Technology:
Enterprise Architecture Assessment Framework*, Version 3.1 (June 2009), and Federal
CIO Council, *Federal Segment Architecture Methodology (FSAM)*, Version 1.0 (Dec. 8,
2008).

Appendix II: Comments from the Department of Health and Human Services

DEPARTMENT OF HEALTH & HUMAN SERVICES   OFFICE OF THE SECRETARY

Assistant Secretary for Legislation
Washington, DC 20201

MAR 7 2012

Valerie C. Melvin, Director
Information Management and Technology Resources Issues
U.S. Government Accountability Office
441 G Street NW
Washington, DC 20548

Dear Ms. Melvin:

Attached are comments on the U.S. Government Accountability Office's (GAO) report entitled, "Information Technology: FDA Needs to Fully Implement Key Management Practices to Lessen Modernization Risks" (GAO-12-346).

The Department appreciates the opportunity to review this draft section of the report prior to publication.

Sincerely,

Jim R. Esquea
Assistant Secretary for Legislation

Attachment

**GENERAL COMMENTS OF THE DEPARTMENT OF HEALTH AND HUMAN
SERVICES (HHS) ON THE GOVERNMENT ACCOUNTABILITY OFFICE'S (GAO)
DRAFT REPORT ENTITLED, "INFORMATION TECHNOLOGY: FDA NEEDS TO
FULLY IMPLEMENT KEY MANAGEMENT PRACTICES TO LESSEN
MODERNIZATION RISKS" (GAO-12-346)**

Over the last several years, FDA has undertaken an important initiative to modernize its information technology (IT) infrastructure and systems in order to optimize the agency's ability to meet its public health mission. The complexity and scale of this ambitious undertaking have compelled the agency to plan this transformation as a multi-phase effort. FDA now has completed phase 1 of the transformation process, which involved modernizing the data center to provide an advanced computing infrastructure that is secure, scalable, flexible and reliable. It provides cloud computing, a concept in which infrastructure, applications, and business processes are delivered to FDA as services, through virtualization over the agency's network, reducing the need for space, time, power and costs. As a result of this initiative, FDA now has a production data center with a secure computing environment that is reliable and able to meet the agency's mission while expanding capacity and agility, allowing FDA to utilize equipment and support resources much more efficiently. To support FDA's bioinformatics initiatives, the agency also has established a high-performance computing enclave, a protected environment that provides the infrastructure to support and strengthen complex data computing and analysis capabilities. FDA's new data center already meets or exceeds all 2012 and 2013 Executive Order and Department of Health and Human Services (HHS) green computing, consolidation, cloud computing and virtualization targets.

The infrastructure modernization and consolidation described above serves as the foundation for all other transformation activities. With this first phase now complete, FDA is in a position to move forward with phase 2: implementing data center operation management and service contract efficiencies while working on modernizing and consolidating software systems with similar business processes and expediting the retirement of legacy systems.

As part of the agency's plan to move forward with phase 2 of its information technology (IT) transformation, and to help integrate the FDA business/regulatory community and its IT support services, in October 2011, FDA created the dual position of and hired a Chief Information Officer (CIO) and Chief Scientist for Informatics. Since his arrival, the agency is undergoing a shift in focus, from Center driven projects to a mix of essential agency level capabilities. Within this new framework, FDA will work with the Centers to modernize and integrate the informatics capabilities across the agency.

The agency has made significant progress in addressing many of the issues that GAO has highlighted in its report. The CIO and Chief Scientist for Informatics now is a member of the Commissioner's Senior Executive Team, which has agreed to govern FDA's IT portfolio at its level. Having now obtained this commitment, the agency is actively working to achieve the first cross-agency, prioritized portfolio. In addition, FDA has established a process to seek feedback from FDA's Senior Executive Team and FDA staff on what is working and needs improvement in the area of IT.

<u>**GENERAL COMMENTS OF THE DEPARTMENT OF HEALTH AND HUMAN
SERVICES (HHS) ON THE GOVERNMENT ACCOUNTABILITY OFFICE'S (GAO)
DRAFT REPORT ENTITLED, "INFORMATION TECHNOLOGY: FDA NEEDS TO
FULLY IMPLEMENT KEY MANAGEMENT PRACTICES TO LESSEN
MODERNIZATION RISKS" (GAO-12-346)**</u>

The Senior Executive Team has conducted several offsite sessions to identify the top 5 – 10
capabilities that are needed for FDA to transform from a domestic agency operating in a globalized
world to a global agency fully prepared for the challenges of its globalized regulatory environment.
Furthermore, to assist in the management of IT investments, FDA's Office of Information
Management (OIM) is in the process of establishing a new Project Management Office to provide
effective, client based services that are aligned with the strategic priorities of the agency.

As part of its systems modernization phase, FDA has initiated several large program/project
reviews. These reviews are focused on identifying areas for improvement, stream-lining large
initiatives into smaller components that can realize success, and determining what projects should
be stopped, continued or started. To date, the agency has evaluated two major programs in-depth.
FDA has halted Janus, an initiative to manage FDA structured scientific data about FDA-regulated
products. FDA also is conducting a detailed process assessment of the Mission Accomplishment
and Regulatory Compliance Services (MARCS) system, a program intended to manage the
integration, reengineering and enhancement of several legacy systems, to determine if it meets the
agency's business needs. FDA also is revising the draft IT Strategic Plan to provide focus, and is
working to define and implement its enterprise architecture model, the framework it uses to manage
and align FDA's IT assets with its operational characteristics.

In addition, FDA now is moving toward agile software development and open source solutions.
Agile processes are more people oriented, adaptive, and flexible than traditional methods which
emphasize rigid plans and detailed documentation. They enable software development as an
iterative process with flexibility for change as business processes evolve. Agile development also is
useful for managing large projects through incremental stages, breaking them down to more
manageable pieces that can be completed and used even as the larger system is being developed.
Open source solutions leverage software that is publicly available, save costs, and allow for the
allocation of resources toward the development of systems that cannot be accessed through open
source channels. FDA also has developed a security/network model that the Health and Human
Services Domain IT Steering Committee and the CIO Council have approved and resourced for
development across HHS.

To meet FDA's needs as it embarks on the IT systems modernization phase, the agency also is
assessing its IT workforce in OIM divisions to identify skill set gaps, develop staff training plans
and identify IT personnel resource needs. FDA has demonstrated its commitment to modernizing
the IT workforce by setting aside training dollars and reviewing and approving staff training plans.
FDA acknowledges that these workforce development activities must be a recurring process in
order to ensure OIM personnel skills keep pace with evolving technologies and methodologies.
Furthermore, FDA's OIM has a strong senior leadership team and is committed to placing
permanent leadership in all remaining acting positions that report directly to the CIO.

2

<u>**GENERAL COMMENTS OF THE DEPARTMENT OF HEALTH AND HUMAN
SERVICES (HHS) ON THE GOVERNMENT ACCOUNTABILITY OFFICE'S (GAO)
DRAFT REPORT ENTITLED, "INFORMATION TECHNOLOGY: FDA NEEDS TO
FULLY IMPLEMENT KEY MANAGEMENT PRACTICES TO LESSEN
MODERNIZATION RISKS" (GAO-12-346)**</u>

FDA has posted job vacancy announcements for all such positions, the announcements have closed,
and FDA is now evaluating the applicants.

In conclusion, the completed infrastructure modernization, coupled with strong leadership and
planning as the agency embarks on systems modernization, provide the foundation for the
sustainable and scalable management practices needed for subsequent phases of FDA's IT
transformation. FDA is committed to transforming its IT environment to advance its public health
mission.

3

Appendix III: Food and Drug Administration IT Mission-Critical Systems and Modernization Initiatives

FDA provided us with the following list of 21 mission-critical systems and modernization initiatives in response to our request for the agency's IT portfolio.

Table 3: FDA Mission-Critical Systems and Modernization Initiatives

Project	Description
Information Computing Technologies for the 21st Century (ICT21) - Data Center Modernization and Migration	Replace FDA's outdated data centers with new production and test facilities, and establish a disaster recovery site.
FDA Advisory Committee Tracking System	Implement a centralized, integrated, and fully electronic system that will significantly reduce current paper processes used to manage FDA advisory committees.
Regulated Product Submission	International effort to develop a single standard for electronic submission of information on regulated products, including food additives, medical devices, and veterinary products to regulatory authorities in FDA and corresponding agencies in other nations.
ICT21 - ARRA Patient Centered Outcomes Research	Effort to integrate standardized data into a data warehouse; conduct cross-trial analysis pilots for detecting clinical trends to understand which interventions are most effective for which patients under specific circumstances; identify pilot studies that shall provide selected structured data sets to external researchers.
Harmonized Inventory	Standardize about 20 IT systems that did not have standardized data and processes; establish and integrate standardized business processes and data elements throughout FDA.
ICT21 - JANUS	Create an informatics system that can rapidly provide FDA staff with the ability to retrieve and analyze data about regulated products using structured scientific data.
FDA Adverse Event Reporting System	Centralize back-end analysis part of adverse event reporting formerly done by the centers. Provides tools to analyze patterns in adverse events for early detection of problems in biologics and drugs and report the results to safeguard the public health.
Automated Laboratory Management	Facilitate communication between labs by creating an electronic environment based on a standardized format.
Common Electronic Document Room[a]	Combine centers' Electronic Document Rooms to contain virtually all documents received and generated by FDA, improve access to those documents and metadata across center lines, and enhance the ability of agency reviewers and others to perform their jobs.
FDA Advanced Submission and Tracking Review[a]	Review new FDA IT systems to identify general-purpose IT components that support the core technical competency of multiple business processes. These IT components are to be reused in future systems to improve the consistency of systems and cost-efficient development.
MedWatch Plus - Safety Reporting Portal	Establish a single portal to collect food and veterinary medicine adverse event information.
Predictive Risk-based Evaluation for Dynamic Import Compliance Targeting (PREDICT)	Create a risk-based import screening tool to improve the efficiency and productivity of the entry review and inspection process through targeting high-risk imports and leveraging automated verification of product compliance with center databases.
Automated Employee Processing[a]	Ease information collection for human capital systems, particularly those where an employee joins, transfers within, or leaves FDA.
FDA Unified Registration and Listing System	The FDA Registration and Listing System that includes Food Facility Registration Module, Center for Drug Evaluation and Research Drug Facility Registration Module, Center for Devices and Radiological Health Device Registration and Listing Module, Alert System, Structured Product Labeling Processing and Routing Services to integrate eList and Firms Master List Services.

Project	Description
Mission Accomplishment and Compliance Regulatory Services (MARCS)	Enhance eight legacy systems with functions including inspecting imports and collecting information on facilities.
FDA Mail/BlackBerry®	Provide Email and BlackBerry® messaging service to the agency
ORA Electronic Laboratory Exchange Network (eLEXNET)	The nation's first Internet-based data exchange system that allows federal, state, and local laboratories to electronically share food safety sample and test data for various food-borne pathogens
ORA Recall Enterprise System	A centralized database for all recall activity that has substantially reduced the time it takes to collect, process, and track recall information. It has also eliminated the need for a variety of hard copy recall recommendation formats
FDA.gov	FDA's public-facing website
Low-Acid Canned Food	Low-Acid Canned Food supports 21 CFR 108 requirements for all foreign and domestic commercial facilities to register and file product processes with FDA
3rd Party Certification Pilot[a]	Gather technical and operational information to assist FDA in determining infrastructure and resource needs, as well as the process for evaluating third-party certification programs, in order to assist FDA in moving toward broader recognition of voluntary third-party recognition systems, including third-party certification programs for aquacultured shrimp.

Source: FDA.

[a]On February 9, 2012, FDA indicated that these initiatives are no longer active.

Appendix IV: FDA IT Investments

The following table provides details on FDA's IT investments, as described in the agency's fiscal year 2013 exhibit 53 submission.

Table 4: FDA IT Investments

Type	Title	Description
Non-major	Center for Biologics Evaluation and Research Prescription Drug User Fee Act Electronic Submission Program	The Electronic Submissions Investment is an integrated system that enables the electronic regulatory process between industry and Center for Biologics Evaluation and Research, Center for Drug Evaluation and Research and Center for Devices and Radiological Health. It stores, retrieves, and distributes submissions to reviewers and interfaces with Center for Biologics Evaluation and Research databases.
Non-major	Center for Biologics Evaluation and Research Prescription Drug User Fee Act Regulatory Management System-Biologics License Application	This investment is an information system for the Center for Biologics Evaluation and Research and the Center for Drug Evaluation and Research to track and report on Biologic License Applications. It was developed to support the Center for Biologics Evaluation and Research's Managed Review Process. This project supports Medical Device User Fee and Modernization Act and Prescription Drug User Fee Act goals.
Non-major	Center for Biologics Evaluation and Research Other Prescription Drug User Fee Act Systems	The Center for Biologics Evaluation and Research Prescription Drug User Fee Act investment consists of systems supporting Lot Release, Pre-Submissions, Investigational New Drug, Investigational Device Exemption, Emergency Use Authorizations, meetings, time, and document tracking. These projects were developed to support the Center for Biologics Evaluation and Research's Managed Review Process and support/financed by the Prescription Drug User Fee Act.
Non-major	Center for Biologics Evaluation and Research Non-Prescription Drug User Fee Act Systems	This investment consists of several projects supporting adverse events reporting, drug and device reviews, biologic product compliance, as well as blood, tissue and Xenotransplantation product registration/adverse events.
Non-major	Office of the Commissioner Unified Registration and Listing System	FDA Unified Registration and Listing System registers food, drug, medical devices and shell egg producer facilities, and supplies infrastructure and account management for Prior Notice of Food Imports and Low-Acid Canned Foods.
Major	Center for Drug Evaluation and Research MedWatch Plus	The MedWatch Plus program is critical to gathering and analysis of the adverse event report information which enables safety monitoring of FDA regulated products, and facilitates expedient corrective actions, in order to protect and promote public health.
Major	Office of Regulatory Affairs Regulatory Business Information Services	Provides data availability and data quality for all of ORA's regulatory activities. The Regulatory Business Information Services support all FDA Field activities including domestics, imports, and enforcement. This includes providing reporting and information on regulated firms.

Type	Title	Description
Major	Office of Regulatory Affairs Mission Accomplishments and Regulatory Compliance Services	The primary IT mechanism for realizing ORA program goals that supports all FDA Field activities (except labs) including domestics, imports, and enforcement. It directly supports the FDA Centers including the Center for Biologics Evaluation and Research, The Center for Drug Evaluation and Research, the Center for Devices and Radiological Health, the Center for Food Safety and Applied Nutrition, and the Center for Veterinary Medicine.
Major	Office of Regulatory Affairs Automated Laboratory Management	Encompasses Quality Management Information System, Electronic Laboratory Exchange Network, and Laboratory Information Management System. It provides for ORA-wide program quality, sample analysis information sharing across the ORA and with external partners, and increased throughput via laboratory automation.
Non-major	Office of the Commissioner Science First	Science First is a web-based knowledge management system that enhances the FDA's science base, necessary for FDA to meet its mission of protecting and promoting the public health.
Non-major	Office of the Commissioner Building Access System	FDA Building Access System investment is state of the art controlled access system monitored 24/7 with card access, intrusion alarms, maps, alarm points, video cameras/recorders, emergency call numbers, and guard tours.
Non-major	Office of Commissioner - Office of Information Management IT Security Program	This investment provides agency strategy, planning, and execution of the requirements set forth under Title III of the E-Government Act of 2002 (Federal Information Security Management Act), the Critical Infrastructure Protection program and HHS/FDA information security program policies.
Non-major	Office of the Commissioner - Office of Information Management IT Governance	FDA IT Governance is composed of the capital planning and investment control, IT investment management, enterprise architecture, workload planning, and related program/project management. The main goal of this investment is to improve the value of IT investments from the business perspective.
Major	Office of the Commissioner User Fee and Financial Reporting Systems	Operates, supports, and enhances three mission-critical systems that collect, manage, and report about $3 billion in user fees mandated by the Prescription Drug User Fee Act, Medical Device User Fee and Modernization Act, Animal Drug User Fee Act, Animal Generic Drug User Fee Act legislation. Interfaces to the HHS Unified Financial Management System for financial reports including some required by Congress.
Non-major	Office of the Commissioner Facility Management System	An integrated solution for facilities management, design, leasing, building operations and maintenance, strategic space planning and forecasting, hoteling, and more. The Facility Management System is an authoritative source for location information for FDA and its Human Resources and Enterprise Administrative Support Environment system.
Non-major	Office of the Commissioner Emergency Operations Network	Emergency Operations Network Incident Management System plays a critical role in strengthening FDA's capability to prepare for and respond to emergencies by providing a web-based connection where accurate real-time data about incidents can be shared.

Type	Title	Description
Non-major	Center for Biologics Evaluation and Research Electronic Gateway	The objective of the E-Submissions Gateway is to enable the receipt of guidance-compliant electronic submissions over the Internet and to integrate the processing of these submissions with the business unit environments.
Non-major	Office of the Commissioner Agency Information Management System	Manages enterprise administrative business processes. There are applications modules to manage processes such as Freedom of Information, Correspondence, and Ethics.
Non-major	Office of the Commissioner Administrative Systems Automation Project	FDA's source data on personnel, organizations, and location information for FDA systems. It combines data from two separate HHS personnel systems and maintains additional data about employees and contractors.
Non-major	National Center for Toxicological Research Methods Development Support	This investment is where software engineers apply IT skills to specific research data-gathering and reporting problems in order to increase throughput and/or enhance the quality and utility of the research data being collected.
Non-major	National Center for Toxicological Research Research Management	This investment provides the essential tools for gathering the data and for providing the necessary decision support mechanisms for the activity-based costing regimen used to allocate available resources for new and ongoing research efforts.
Non-major	National Center for Toxicological Research Research Support	Automate and thus standardize the collection, storage, and reporting of research data by the application of database design, systems development, and reporting techniques and tools, including existing and emerging technologies where appropriate.
Non-major	Center for Veterinary Medicine Integrated Services for Veterinary Medicine	A mixed life-cycle investment supporting premarket, postmarket, product quality, and administrative services activities within the Center for Veterinary Medicine
Non-major	Center for Food Safety and Applied Nutrition Scientific Computing and Application Interface	Includes infrastructure, stakeholder outreach and information dissemination, scientific computing support, and scientific research project management.
Non-major	Center for Food Safety and Applied Nutrition Food Applications Regulatory Management System	A comprehensive end-to-end image-based electronic document management and workflow automation system that provides efficient receipt of applications and expedited safety reviews and decisions and information management and maximizes productivity.
Non-major	Center for Food Safety and Applied Nutrition Supporting and Enabling IT	Provides electronic workflow to automate common business practices of submissions and centralized modules for standardized vocabulary control and administrative functions such as account management, and people and organizational data.
Non-major	Center for Food Safety and Applied Nutrition Certification, Compliance, Monitoring and Enforcement System	Provides IT support to pre- and postmarket business processes through efficient data collection, processing, analysis, and reporting to facilitate the Center for Food Safety and Applied Nutrition's regulatory and compliance activities and e-Gov for business stakeholders.

Type	Title	Description
Non-major	Center for Food Safety and Applied Nutrition Adverse Events Reporting System	A postmarket surveillance system for tracking and analyzing adverse event reports involving foods, cosmetics, infant formula, and dietary supplements to help identify potential public health risks and provide feedback to industry.
Non-major	Center for Devices and Radiological Health Mammography Program Reporting Information System	An automated system that supports the Mammography Quality Standards Act and provides ways to improve the reliability, integrity, and accessibility of mammography facility certification, inspection, and compliance data and permits accurate tracking of mammography information.
Non-major	Center for Devices and Radiological Health Medical Product Surveillance Network	The Medical Product Surveillance Network is a pilot sentinel reporting project designed to improve surveillance and follow-up of medical device adverse events at a sample of user facilities.
Non-major	Center for Devices and Radiological Health Electronic Submission	A document management system and central repository for pre- and postmarket documents. Includes development and implementation of the Center for Devices and Radiological Health's electronic submissions, Center for Veterinary Medicine's electronic submissions and near-term document management needs, the Center for Biologics Evaluation and Research's, and Center for Tobacco Products' electronic submissions.
Major	Center for Drug Evaluation and Research Automated Drug Information Management System	Automated Drug Information Management System is being developed as a fully electronic system to receive, evaluate, and disseminate information about investigational and marketing submissions for human drugs and therapeutic biologics.
Major	Office of the Commissioner – Office of Information Management Information and Computing Technologies for the 21st Century	Initiative to modernize infrastructure for advanced scientific tools and techniques, improve use of analytics, and provide technical capacity for regulatory functions and decisions.
Non-major	Office of the Commissioner Advisory Committee Tracking and Reporting System	The FDA Advisory Committee Tracking System streamlines the following workflows: Federal Register, Conflict of Interest, Committee Charter Management, Committee Member Nomination Management, and annual, quarterly, and unscheduled reporting.
Non-major	Center for Drug Evaluation and Research Harmonized Inventory	Harmonized Inventory is an agencywide initiative to standardize and improve the data quality of firm and product information.
Major	Office of the Commissioner – Office of Information Management Operational Infrastructure	Supports the HHS goals of effective IT management and advancing scientific and biomedical research, and HHS regulatory activities by providing IT infrastructure including voice/data communications, and data center operations and maintenance for the FDA.
Non-major	Office of the Commissioner – Office of Information Management Connect	Regulated Product Submission is an HL7 exchange message that provides FDA the ability to organize, process, and review submissions by defining the framework for regulatory information using predefined parameters to identify and catalog submission information.

Type	Title	Description
Non-major	Center for Tobacco Products Social Media/Knowledge Management	This investment will create a Center for Tobacco Products networking site and collaborative workspace to help manage and transfer knowledge, locate information and experts, and build a community of colleagues.
Non-major	Center for Food Safety and Applied Nutrition Safety Reporting Portal	A new website launched by the National Institutes of Health and FDA for industry to report food safety problems or adverse events involving FDA-regulated foods and animal feeds, pet foods and pet treats, animal drugs, human gene transfer research, and tobacco products.
Non-major	Center for Devices and Radiological Health Submission Tracking And Reporting	A suite of applications, which includes the Center Tracking System and Center for Devices and Radiological Health Ad-Hoc Reporting System, that are critical to meeting the center's regulatory requirements by helping the center track, manage, and report on its work.
Non-major	Center for Devices and Radiological Health Unique Device Identification Database	The Unique Device Identification Database system will aid in improving medical device safety by providing a mechanism for regulated entities subject to unique device identification to submit a core set of device-related identification information to the database.
Non-major	Center for Tobacco Products Electronic Submissions and Business Automation	This investment supports development, implementation, and operations and maintenance of the Center for Tobacco Products' electronic submissions as well as Center for Tobacco Products' current and future business process automation needs.
Non-major	Center for Devices and Radiological Health Premarket Application Modernization	The primary objective of this investment and project is the modernization—in terms of reliability, functionality, quality, and technology—of the Center for Devices and Radiological Health's premarket data entry applications and databases.
Non-major	Center for Devices and Radiological Health Knowledge Management	This initiative includes tasks for establishing knowledge management governance and policies; deploying tools and technology for social business systems; search and discovery, and integration with taxonomies to improve users' ability to find information.

Source: FDA exhibit 53 data.

FDA began the MARCS effort in 2002, and since that time has made several shifts in its approach. At that time, ORA envisioned that the program would replace its two key legacy systems, the Operational Administrative System for Import Support (OASIS) and the Field Accomplishments and Compliance Tracking System (FACTS). Since 2002, the program's requirements were changed and broadened to include replacement of six additional legacy systems. In April 2005, FDA developed a design that envisioned a set of integrated service components intended to provide the applications and tools to support the agency's import operations, field operations, compliance operations, firm management, workload management, and selected aspects of laboratory operations. The agency estimated that development would cost about $75 million and be completed in 2008.

However, later in 2005, a decision was made to put the current vision for the program on hold, and instead implement web-enabled versions of OASIS and FACTS. According to an Office of Information Management (OIM) supervisory IT specialist, the migration to web-enabled systems allowed the agency to implement single sign-on and enabled the legacy systems to integrate more easily with new functionality. According to the Program Manager and contract officials, the decision to implement web-enabled versions was also motivated by vendor plans to halt support for the current OASIS and FACTS platform and uncertainty about funding for the program.

In April 2006, FDA rebaselined the program estimate to include development costs and maintenance costs for the entire program life cycle. FDA estimated that the total life-cycle cost would be $221.4 million, and the investment would end in August 2019. It estimated that development would cost $113.8 million, and most development would be complete by November 2012.

According to the Program Manager and contract officials, between 2006 and 2009, FDA's work included the following:

- In 2006, migration of OASIS and FACTS to a web-enabled version was completed.

- In May 2007, the program was rebaselined again with a slight increase in development costs to $115 million.

- In 2008, migration to a new operating system, UNIX, was completed.

- In late 2008, the agency began development of the Predictive Risk-
  based Evaluation for Dynamic Import Compliance Targeting
  (PREDICT), intended to replace the automated import admissibility
  screening module of OASIS, which relied on direct inputs of rules,
  providing risk ranking, automated database lookups, and warnings in
  the case of data anomalies or likely violations.

- During this time, additional legacy systems were planned for inclusion
  in the program, and the agency also developed some of the support
  services envisioned such as firm management and a document
  repository.

In 2009, the collection of legacy systems planned for the program was
based on a wide variety of disparate technologies with redundant and
inconsistent data. According to officials, the program received multiyear
funding to resume development of the system based on the design from
2005. FDA awarded a master integrator contract in late 2009 for
incremental development of MARCS by a single integrator. In May 2009,
the agency rebaselined the program to accelerate delivery of functionality
and include PREDICT. FDA's rebaselined estimate for the life-cycle cost
was $253.6 million with development costs of $143.3 million, based on
completing most development in September 2014. According to FDA, in
2010, the agency updated and revalidated the program's requirements.

According to OMB exhibit 53s from 2004 to 2013, FDA has spent
approximately $160 million from fiscal year 2002 to fiscal year 2011 on
MARCS. Figure 4 shows these expenditures, as well as enacted
spending for fiscal year 2012.

Figure 4: MARCS Expenditures, Fiscal Years 2002-2012

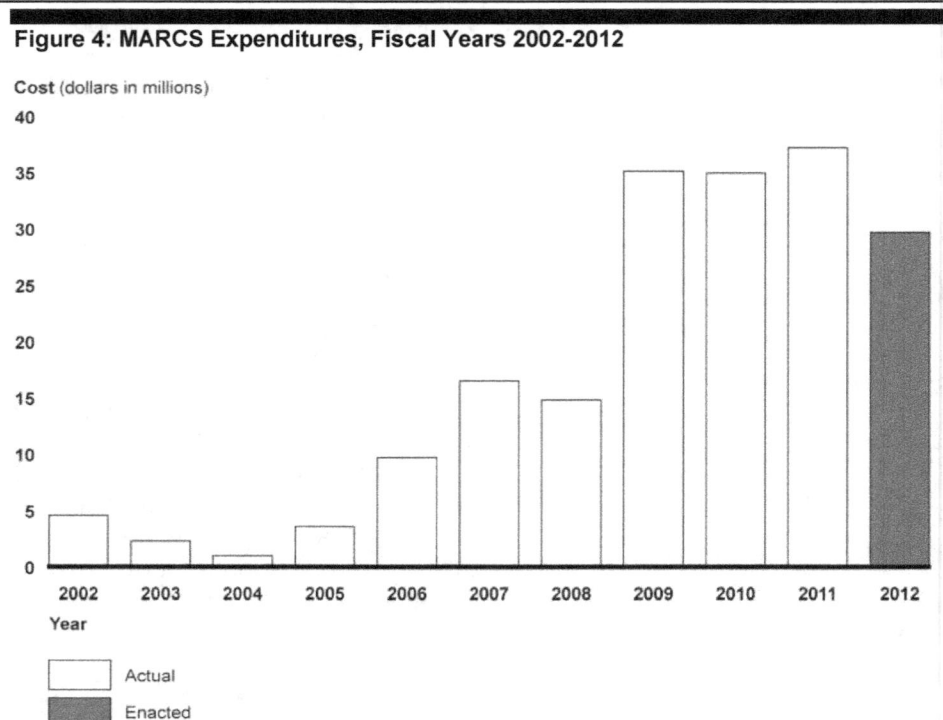

Source: GAO analysis of OMB data.

Note: The scope of the MARCS program expenditures changed over time. According to FDA, prior to
2009, expenditures included primarily operations and maintenance and some development,
modernization, and enhancement for legacy systems. In 2009, FDA awarded a contract for design,
development and implementation of MARCS. FDA also said that prior to 2009, the agency considered
funding for MARCS to be low.

In August 2011, FDA again rebaselined the program estimates to account for new legislative and regulatory requirements based on the FDA Food Safety Modernization Act.[1] It estimated that the total life-cycle cost will be $282.7 million[2] and planned to deploy a significant portion of MARCS and retire its legacy systems by July 2014. Table 5 provides details on the program estimates over time.

---

[1]Pub. L. No. 111-353, Jan. 4, 2011.

[2]MARCS life-cycle costs of $282.7 million include FDA's August 2011 rebaseline request for additional funding required to meet the changes for the FDA Food Safety Modernization Act. These funds were not previously included in the fiscal year 2012 OMB exhibit 300.

Table 5: MARCS Rebaselines

	April 2005	April 2006	May 2007	May 2009	August 2011
MARCS total cost estimate	Not estimated	$221.4 million	$222.5 million	$253.6 million	$282.7 million
Investment completion date	Not estimated	August 2019	September 2019	September 2019	September 2019
Steady state costs	Not estimated	$107.6 million	$107.5 million	$110.3 million	$105.0 million
Development, modernization, and enhancement costs	$75 million	$113.8 million	$115.0 million	$143.3 million	$177.7 million
Initial development completion date	September 2008	November 2012	November 2012	September 2014	October 2016

Source: GAO analysis of FDA data.

Appendix VI: Center for Food Safety and Applied Nutrition IT Systems Investments

To fulfill its regulatory mission, FDA's CFSAN relies on various information systems. According to FDA documentation and interviews with agency officials, the center funds 21 databases and their associated systems. These systems fall into seven major categories such as registration, regulatory management, and adverse events. The following table provides details on the seven categories and a brief description of the systems that comprise them.

Table 6: CFSAN IT systems investments

CFSAN investment category	Number of systems and databases	Description of systems and databases
CFSAN Adverse Events Reporting System	1	
	CFSAN Adverse Events Reporting System	The center management tool for voluntary adverse event and product problems reports for all CFSAN-regulated products and mandatory reports of serious adverse events on dietary supplements.
	Arc Geographic Information Systems and Empirica Signal Detection are part of the CFSAN Adverse Events Reporting System	CFSAN plans to use this system to track public health indicators, identify disease clusters, explore sites of environmental risk, and identify spatial patterns and relationships.
		Empirica Signal Detection is used to identify, organize, and interpret food and cosmetic adverse event patterns in the CFSAN Adverse Events Reporting System database.
Food Application Regulatory Management	1	Supports the processing and management of petitions and notifications. These submissions address chemical, toxicological, environmental and other issues regarding specific ingredients, and are the basis for the regulatory safety decisions.
	Food Application Regulatory Management	
Certification, Compliance, Monitoring, and Enforcement Systems	8	
	Seafood Hazard Analysis Critical Control Point	An online web-based system that processes domestic and foreign seafood inspection data from ORA Field Inspectors and state partners.
	Interstate Milk Shippers	Provides a central repository for FDA Regional Milk Specialists to electronically submit inspection data on milk shippers and container manufacturers for review and evaluation.
	Shellfish Shippers	Shellfish Shippers is an online electronic data submission system for State Control Authority Shellfish Shipper inspectors to submit to FDA Interstate Shellfish Dealer's Certificate.
	Retail Food Reference System	A searchable online database of current and historical retail food safety interpretations and opinions.
	Color Batch Certification	Color Batch Certification tracks the processing of the safety review of color certification batch analyses and maintains all color certification records.
	Voluntary Cosmetics Registration Program	Provides information to FDA on the identification of cosmetic establishments and cosmetic formulations.
	Low-Acid Canned Foods	Low-Acid Canned Foods supports 21 CFR 108 requirements for all foreign and domestic Low-Acid Canned Foods/ Acid Foods commercial facilities.
	Small Business Nutrition Labeling Exemption System	Provides an electronic process to meet the Small Business Nutrition Labeling Exemption Notice requirements which allow small businesses with a low product volume to be exempt from FDA's nutrition labeling requirements unless a health or nutrient claim is made.

CFSAN investment category	Number of systems and databases	Description of systems and databases
Scientific Computing and Application Interface	3	
	Scientific Computing and Infrastructure Programs	Supports the generation, access, analysis, storage, transmission, and security of scientific data.
	Priority-based Assessment of Food Additive	A data repository containing over 30 years of summary data on the toxicological effects of direct food ingredients and color additives and a pre- and postmarket review tool that incorporates computational toxicology.
	Chemical Evaluation and Risk Estimation System	A centralized data bank that incorporates and expands on existing databases (Priority-based Assessment of Food Additive, Leadscope, CFSAN Thesaurus, etc) and a pre- and postmarket review tool that incorporates computational toxicology.
Supporting and Enabling IT	4	
	Resource Reporting System Via Project	The center planning and reporting tool for employee and resource management.
	Terminology Management System	An FDA-wide licensed tool to control/standardize vocabularies across systems and enable enterprise searching of disparate data collections.
	CFSAN Automated Submission Process Exchange and Reporting	An electronic workflow tracking and information system designed to automate tracking, and processing of submissions across organizations.
	Component Automated Research Tracking System	The official information repository and principal research program coordination and communications tool for FDA's Foods and Veterinary Medicine Program and includes the portfolio for food-, feed-, veterinary medicine-, and cosmetics-related research being conducted and/or funded by CFSAN, the Center for Veterinary Medicine, and ORA.
FDA Unified Registration and Listing System	3	
	Food Facility Registration Module	Provides an electronic means to register all facilities including foreign facilities that manufacture, process or hold food items that are sold for consumption in the United States.
	Shell Egg Producer Registration Module	Provides a means for egg farm producers to register their farms electronically and for both CFSAN and ORA Field personnel to conduct inspections of egg farms and allocate inspection resources.
	Certificates Application Processing	Automates the processing of CFSAN export certificates and collects user fees under FDA Unified Registration and Listing System.
Safety Reporting Portal (Partnership with National Institutes of Health)	1	
	Safety Reporting Portal	Supports voluntary and mandatory reporting of reportable food reports, pet food and animal drug adverse events.

Source: FDA.

Appendix VII: GAO Contact and Staff Acknowledgments

GAO Contact	Valerie C. Melvin, (202) 512-6304 or melvinv@gao.gov
Staff Acknowledgments	In addition to the contact named above, key contributions were made to this report by Christie Motley, Assistant Director; Neil Doherty; Anh Le; Jason Lee; J. Chris Martin; Lee McCracken; Umesh Thakkar; Daniel Wexler; Merry Woo; and Charles Youman.

GAO's Mission	The Government Accountability Office, the audit, evaluation, and investigative arm of Congress, exists to support Congress in meeting its constitutional responsibilities and to help improve the performance and accountability of the federal government for the American people. GAO examines the use of public funds; evaluates federal programs and policies; and provides analyses, recommendations, and other assistance to help Congress make informed oversight, policy, and funding decisions. GAO's commitment to good government is reflected in its core values of accountability, integrity, and reliability.
Obtaining Copies of GAO Reports and Testimony	The fastest and easiest way to obtain copies of GAO documents at no cost is through GAO's website (www.gao.gov). Each weekday afternoon, GAO posts on its website newly released reports, testimony, and correspondence. To have GAO e-mail you a list of newly posted products, go to www.gao.gov and select "E-mail Updates."
Order by Phone	The price of each GAO publication reflects GAO's actual cost of production and distribution and depends on the number of pages in the publication and whether the publication is printed in color or black and white. Pricing and ordering information is posted on GAO's website, http://www.gao.gov/ordering.htm.
	Place orders by calling (202) 512-6000, toll free (866) 801-7077, or TDD (202) 512-2537.
	Orders may be paid for using American Express, Discover Card, MasterCard, Visa, check, or money order. Call for additional information.
Connect with GAO	Connect with GAO on Facebook, Flickr, Twitter, and YouTube. Subscribe to our RSS Feeds or E-mail Updates. Listen to our Podcasts. Visit GAO on the web at www.gao.gov.
To Report Fraud, Waste, and Abuse in Federal Programs	Contact: Website: www.gao.gov/fraudnet/fraudnet.htm E-mail: fraudnet@gao.gov Automated answering system: (800) 424-5454 or (202) 512-7470
Congressional Relations	Katherine Siggerud, Managing Director, siggerudk@gao.gov, (202) 512-4400, U.S. Government Accountability Office, 441 G Street NW, Room 7125, Washington, DC 20548
Public Affairs	Chuck Young, Managing Director, youngc1@gao.gov, (202) 512-4800 U.S. Government Accountability Office, 441 G Street NW, Room 7149 Washington, DC 20548